POLICE PERSONNEL ADMINISTRATION

POLICE PERSONNEL ADMINISTRATION

By

V. A. LEONARD, B. S., M. S., Ph. D.

Professor Emeritus of Police Administration
Washington State University
Pullman, Washington

CHARLES C THOMAS • PUBLISHER
Springfield • Illinois • U.S.A.

Published and Distributed Throughout the World by

CHARLES C THOMAS • PUBLISHER
301-327 East Lawrence Avenue, Springfield, Illinois, U.S.A.
NATCHEZ PLANTATION HOUSE
735 North Atlantic Boulevard, Fort Lauderdale, Florida, U.S.A.

© *1970, by* CHARLES C THOMAS • PUBLISHER

Library of Congress Catalog Card Number: 75-91852 ✓

With THOMAS BOOKS *careful attention is given to all details of
manufacturing and design. It is the Publisher's desire to present
books that are satisfactory as to their physical qualities and artistic
possibilities and appropriate for their particular use.* THOMAS
BOOKS *will be true to those laws of quality that assure a good
name and good will.*

Printed in the United States of America
KK-4

By the same author:

Police Communication Systems
Survey and Reorganization of the
  Seattle Police Department
Police Organization and Management
  First and Second Editions
A Guide to the Study of Police Organization
  and Management
The Police of the 20th Century
The General Administration of Criminal
  Justice (co-author)
Police Science for the Young American
The Police, the Judiciary and the Criminal
The Police Enterprise—Its Organization
  and Management

PREFACE

T HIS book was written in the interest of successful personnel administration in the smaller police departments of this country. The American police service has passed through a period of transition and has now entered a new era in terms of its most vital resource—personnel. The time is now close at hand when the best in police practice and procedure will be brought to the doorstep of every police officer in the nation.

The new era finds expression on two major fronts: legislation at the state level prescribing minimum selection and training standards for entry into police service, and the emergence of professional police training curricula in the universities and colleges of this country. Both events sharpen the focus on the American police field as a career service for young men and women.

Police Personnel Administration is concerned with these important developments, together with other phases of personnel administration, and their application to the police enterprise in the smaller community.

Chapter I is devoted to the qualifications of police personnel, including the chief of police and his officers. Police entrance qualifications receive appropriate attention, including the age, height and weight requirements, physical and mental condition, intelligence, educational achievement, aptitudes and character. The fallacies of the residence requirement are exposed.

Chapter II examines the mechanics of selection. Considered in turn, are the search for candidates, coordinated statewide recruiting, the application form, audit of applications, the written examination, psychiatric screening of police applicants, the physical and agility test, and background investigation. Other elements of the recruiting process are also presented, including the probationary period and the rating of police personnel. The police cadet system as a recruiting device is considered, together with the role of personnel records and a frank examination of the police salary structure.

In Chapter III, the police training project is treated in detail, including recruit in-service training, curriculum content, Departmental and regional police in-service training schools. The section on legislation at the state level prescribing minimum police selection and training standards, includes an examination of Selection and Training Council Acts now in operation in the states of New York, California, New Jersey and Oregon. The Model Police Standards Council Act drafted by the International Association of Chiefs of Police is also presented.

In this chapter, appropriate attention is given to refresher training, unit or divisional training, the training of supervisory and command personnel, and administrative officers, roll call training, teaching methods and the departmental police library. It is also concerned with the implications for the smaller department of professional police training at the university and college level, together with an evaluation of the joint roles of university police training and the police in-service training program.

Supporting elements in police personnel administration are presented in Chapter IV. They include the lateral mobility of police personnel, the role of women and the use of civilians in the smaller department, conditions of service, fringe benefits, and the police retirement system.

Police Personnel Administration is designed as a manual and convenient reference work for the chief and his officers in the smaller department. In addition, it should prove useful as a training tool in local police training programs and in regional in-service training schools. It should also qualify for a place on the shelves of the personal library of individual police officers.

V. A. L.

CONTENTS

5101

POLICE PERSONNEL ADMINISTRATION

I

THE QUALIFICATIONS OF POLICE PERSONNEL

T HE personnel resources of a police department are its greatest asset. All the way, from the top to the bottom of the enterprise, the calibre of personnel sets the stage for standards of performance in the delivery of police service. The degree of intelligence, zeal, determination and devotion to duty that a police officer brings to roll call as he prepares for his tour of duty, is determined in advance by recruiting standards at the intake.

The Police Chief Executive

First in importance in terms of police personnel management are the qualifications and selection of the chief of police. No greater responsibility confronts the appointing power in local government than the choice of the individual who is to be given control over police administration. It is important, therefore, to consider the qualifications of a chief of police capable of leading his force on the road to success in the effective delivery of police service to the community.

All that has been said concerning leadership capability and the dominance of an idea, applies with compelling force to the police chief executive.[1] As one goes up the scale of supervision and command through the ranks of sergeant, lieutenant and captain to the chief of police, emphasis is placed increasingly on judgment, self-reliance, resourcefulness and leadership potential. The scope of duties gradually broadens and planning in advance expands in importance as the approach is made to the chief himself. He is the chief strategist and the one who is responsible for the operation of the enterprise.

It has been assumed on occasion that the man who has the longest period of service or if several are approximately equal on

---

[1]Leonard, V. A.: *The Police Enterprise — Its Organization and Management,* Thomas, Springfield, Illinois, 1969.

this point, then the man with the best record as a police or detective, may confidently be expected to turn in an outstanding performance as Chief of Police. As early as 1921, Fosdick commented on the fallacy of this point of view:[2]

> The chances are rather that he is unfitted for the task. Lacking in administrative experience, with scant appreciation of the larger possibilities of the position, and often indeed without imagination or resourcefulness, he has little chance of success, and it would be unwise and cruel to saddle him with the responsibility. If police management were merely a matter of assignments, promotions and discipline; if it had to do only with the ordering of a well-defined routine, any capable man who had been through the mill might well be adapted to handle it.
>
> But the task is so much broader than routine, and involves activities of such consequence that only a high order of creative intelligence can cope with it. The executive must deal with community problems in the large. He must be familiar with the underlying social forces which are responsible for the need of police service. . . . He must be able to interpret public opinion, to be a community leader, and above all, he must be qualified to inspire a force of police officers. In addition, he must have a thorough understanding of the principles of administraiton. These qualifications are not easily found in any walk of life.

It is characteristic of many European police forces to go outside the department to select their police administrators. The present Commissioner of Scotland Yard is the first to rise to that high position through the ranks of the department. During a tour of the Belgian police services, the author learned that in the police department of Brussels not only the police chief executive, but all supervisory and command personnel above the rank of sergeant were recruited from outside the department. It was explained that the altogether inadequate salary scale for patrolmen and the resulting low quality of personnel recruited into the patrol services precluded any possibility of having in the patrol ranks individuals who were qualified for promotion. The head of the Brussels police training school expressed the view that when salary structures were

---

[2]Fosdick, Raymond B.: *Police Administration,* Part III of the Cleveland Foundation Survey of Criminal Justice in Cleveland, 1921, pp. 16-17.

adjusted to attract to the patrol services a higher type of individual, external recruiting would be abandoned.

There are few instances in American police history of laymen being appointed as chiefs of police. Notable among these has been the occasional appointment of a ranking military officer as head of a state police organization. The comparative success of such men in positions of police management is understandable because of the close parallel between military and police operations.

Lay management of a police organization with its inherent limitations may be observed where administrative control of both police and fire departments is lodged in a commissioner of public safety, as in the commission plan of municipal government. These officials have seldom had either experience or training in the police field, with the result that in addition to the evils of plural command, inexperience and professional incompetence interfere with the successful operation of a police department.

Basic, then, among the qualifications of the police executive is an extended and successful experience in police service, characterized preferably by assignment to every rank in the department. The knowledge gained firsthand concerning the problems of the patrolman, the sergeant, the lieutenant and the captain, add to the capacity for management of the police enterprise. Armed with a technical knowledge of the functions and problems of the various staff and line units of police organization, he is in a position to weigh their relative importance in the equation of crime control, and to integrate their joint effort toward immediate and long-term police objectives.

Method of Selection

The method of selection by which the police administrator is brought into office has an important bearing upon the quality of management. The manner in which the appointing officer determines who is best fitted for the responsibilities of a chief of police is a matter of considerable consequence.

It is quite apparent that empirical methods involving merely off-hand judgment and "horse sense" are not the answer. Even if the appointing power is bent upon the selection of the most capable man available for the position, some form of screening process bearing the stamp of scientific sanction is necessary in order to forecast as far as possible the probable success of the candidate as he takes over the reins of management. It follows that examination techniques in one form or another should be brought into play as a part of the screening process in order to evaluate the extent to which the candidate possesses those qualifications admittedly desirable in a police adminstrator.

The trend in the American community, regardless of size, is toward an open competitive examination which is not limited to personnel in the department concerned. The City of Seattle, on a consultant's recommendation,[3] amended its charter and held a national open competitive examination for the position of chief of police. The elimination of residence requirements and abolition of tenure coterminous with the mayor operated in attracting to the competition men of demonstrated ability.

Approximately one hundred applications were received. After an audit of applications, forty-six candidates, representing some of the best administrative talent in the American police field, competed in the examination. The outstanding record of the Seattle Police Department under Chief George D. Eastman's administration more than vindicated the decision of the people in that community to select their police chief executive by open competitive examination. The official announcement of the examination and the application form shown in Appendix A, give convincing evidence of a new trend in the selection of police administrators.

An increasing number of American cities in various population groups are now following this tested procedure in the selection of their chiefs of police. The police in the smaller communities and the people they serve stand to make important gains in the quality of police service through the use of this method.

---

[3]Leonard, V. A.: *Survey and Reorganization of the Seattle Police Department,* 1946, p. 40.
See Appendix A for copy of examination announcement and application form which were given nationwide circulation.

As previously indicated, the competitive examination should not be limited to personnel in the department concerned. In order to extend the field of selection, examination announcements should at least be distributed throughout the state in which the community is located. If considered necessary, the cooperation of police personnel officers in nearby cities or in the state police in developing examination procedure, would be available for the asking.

Police Personnel Selection

Fundamental to successful police service in the smaller community is the individual police officer, selected with care and well-trained for the job. The patrolman of today is the sergeant, the lieutenant, the captain, the chief of police of tomorrow. Thus, the character of police service is almost completely determined by personnel policy and very largely at the intake by recruiting standards. Police chiefs and other officials of local government are recognizing this basic principle and as a result, recruiting standards are moving upward in order to attract to police service career-minded young men and women.

Conscientious police executives know that the quality and quantity of police service is not determined to any impressive degree by sheer numerical strength alone. Recognition of that fact is bringing the problems of police recruitment and training into sharp focus. Management in the police field is becoming personnel conscious. It has been demonstrated that the intelligence, training, mental health and career interests of the individual officer can combine with good organization and management to produce a police force with superior capabilities.

Police Entrance Qualifications

A satisfactory personnel program in any enterprise requires the establishment of entrance standards that will bring into the service men and women equipped to meet successfully the tasks they will be called upon to perform. The most critical stage in police personnel administration is that of recruitment, for it is at that point that the calibre of the force is determined.

This concept received early recognition in the organization of state police systems and in all probability explains their frequent superiority to municipal police forces. The first state police executives were military leaders. These men were trained to the belief that the proper selection of a man for a given job was fundamental, and they carried this idea over into their methods of choosing men for the state police force. The fear in which characters of the underworld hold state police forces, and the respect in which these officers are held by the general public, is a tribute to the careful selection and training these forces have received.

Prevailing entrance requirements in the municipal services of this country may be stated in general as follows:

Age .... 21 to 31 years
Height .... 5′ 8″ to 5′ 10″ (in stocking feet)
Weight .... 150 lbs. or more
Education .... Grammar school to high school or equivalent
Physical condition ..... Good health and freedom from any major physical defect
Character .... No previous criminal record
Residence .... Requirement varies

The above requirements will vary somewhat from one department to another but may be regarded as a cross-section or average of entrance qualifications in the American police services today. Some departments are less exact in this respect than others, and wherever this is true, the people of the communities they serve suffer a corresponding reduction in the quality of police protection. It is desirable at this point to comment further on each one of the foregoing qualifications.

The Age Requirement. The prevailing age limits for induction into police service were, for many years, twenty-three to thirty-five years. There has been an observable trend during the past few years toward a reduction in both limits. The younger man is more flexible and therefore, more easy to mold to the aims, ideals and accepted practices of the department. They learn easier and faster in the police training school. They possess more vigor, energy and alertness than the older man and are not likely to have had their initiative stifled by some previous job failure.

From the standpoint of personnel turnover, if the candidate has not already firmly established himself in some trade, he is less likely to leave the department when industrial production is at its peak and jobs are plentiful. The career-minded man is the young man. Insistence upon youth in recruiting police officers is generally found wherever successful police departments are maintained.

Today, the age of twenty-one years is widely considered as the absolute minimum limit for entry into police service on the questionable basis that this is the age at which the young man first attains legally the status of manhood. So far as police objectives and the means for achieving them are concerned, mental age is of far greater importance than chronological age, and it offers a more scientific basis than minimum age requirements.

There is strong testimony for fixing the maximum age limit no more than twenty-five years, and there is strong evidence to indicate that men between the minimum age limit and twenty-five make the best material for policemen. They learn quicker and make better records in the police training academy than do men who are past twenty-five years of age. In addition, it is important to observe that the more nearly the age of the applicant approaches thirty, the more likely it is that he has failed at everything he has tried.

The Height Requirement. An examination of many entrance qualification schedules in American police departments reveals a height range from five feet five inches to six feet six inches. The small man is invaluable at times in police service, but there is a psychological advantage that goes with the larger man in the control of people, singly or in groups, that is generally not overlooked. Most departments have arrived at the average of five feet ten inches in height. Obviously, there is no correlation between height and intelligence, which leads all other factors in qualifying for police service.

The Weight Requirement. Where formerly 200 pounds of brawn constituted the primary requirement for service in a police uniform, the weight factor now is only of nominal significance. The requirement today will vary somewhat from one department to another, but most departments agree upon a minimum of 150 pounds. A reasonable and safe procedure is to consider weight in proportion to height. There is an observable tendency among American police departments to place greater emphasis upon physical and mental health than upon height and weight.

Physical and Mental Condition. The candidate must possess robust physical health in every respect, as determined by a competent doctor of medicine. Equally important, reliable determinations must be made with respect to mental health, personality, nervous condition, temperament, social intellect, habits and ideals. The services of a psychiatrist in making these evaluations for the police in the smaller community, are usually available nearby.

The time and cost involved in appraising physical and mental condition may seem out of proportion to their importance. But experience has proven otherwise in those departments where the exercise of rigid precautions in this respect has lowered personnel turnover and brought about other economies in administration which more than offset the additional expense. On the credit side of the ledger also is the enhanced personal performance on the job of men who can meet these standards.

The same considerations which dictate a rigid physical examination for all candidates suggest the necessity of annual physical examinations for all departmental personnel. From the standpoint of preventive medicine, incipient difficulties may be discovered and proper remedial measures taken at a time when they can produce the best results. Such examinations serve the interests of both the officer and the department.

A candidate who is in doubtful health should be rejected. In addition to the liability of sub-standard performance, he may become a pensioner in a short time with the necessity of replacing him, and with the result that two men are carried on the payroll for the rest of their lives rather than one. Days lost on account of sickness in American police departments continue as a serious drain on effective personnel strength and add tremendously to the cost of police protection in this country.

Physical Strength and Agility. Both physical strength and agility should be required of the police applicant to a superior degree. Appropriate tests designed to measure these qualities may be obtained from the department of physical education at any nearby college or university.

Intelligence. Admittedly, the person possessing an absorbing interest in his chosen field may be able to overcome intellectual deficiencies and deliver a passable performance. It is extremely doubtful, however, that there ever was a *successful* policeman who was not unusually intelligent. In some positions a person with limited mental equipment may make a good showing, but in police service there appears to be a level beyond which a police officer cannot go unless he has superior mental equipment. Interest, initiative and a dynamic personality may carry some persons up the promotional ladder, but it does not follow that they have the capability to fill their positions adequately after they have reached the higher levels.

The highest degree of intelligence available is none too good for the trying tasks that daily confront a police officer. The organizational chain is no stronger than its weakest link, and the stupid, blundering individual, who by his acts can bring discredit upon an entire organization, becomes the public's measuring stick for the whole department. One inferior man who fails to rise to an emergency can prejudice the reputation of an otherwise excellent police force.

Rapid and accurate thinking is an essential quality of the police officer. He must reach decisions concerning the application of the law without delay, and he must make no errors in arriving at his decision because the public is always the "second guesser."

A New York City police officer made a split-second decision on one occasion and it later took the State Supreme Court six months to decide whether he was right or wrong. An officer's perceptive powers, his imagination, his ability to concentrate his attention upon the tasks that are before him, his memory—visual and auditory—and his reasoning and judgment, must all be of the best. Otherwise, the individual must fail when confronted with some of the crucial tests that are the lot of every police officer. Furthermore, a high order of intelligence is necessary if the new recruit is to absorb readily the material submitted in the police training program.

Police entrance standards must provide for the selection of men possessing a superior degree of intelligence in order to assure satisfactory performance in positions to which the officer may later advance. A minimum intelligence quotient of 112 is recognized by leaders in the field for entry into police service. With the trend toward a minimum educational standard of two years preparation at the university and college level, the minimum IQ is virtually set automatically. An individual with less than this rating would experience difficulty in completing course work at the university level. Since entrance requirements in colleges and universities are being raised continuously, it is possible that a minimum intelligence quotient of from 115 to 120 may become the standard for entry into police service.

Educational Background. Educational requirements in American police departments vary from the ability to read and write to high-school graduation, with the trend definitely toward the requirement of a university degree in the police science major. Accidental infiltration of men with university training into the police services has escaped the attention of most observers. As early as 1945, in one police department with a total personnel strength of 628, there were eighty-four individuals possessing from two to eight years of university training. The head of one division in this department was the holder of a Phi Beta Kappa key.

This development may be attributed in part to a rise in average educational levels among the total populations. However, it is undoubtedly true that the complex nature of the police task and the march toward professionalization in the police services have operated as factors in challenging the interest of college-trained men and women.

It probably would not be in error to assume that today, close

to 10 per cent of the total personnel in American police departments possess from one to four years of university training. This
infiltration, although proceeding for the most part unnoticed,
marks a significant turning point in American police history. The
performance record of these men is paving the way for formal
elevation of educational standards as a part of the qualifications
for police service. Furthermore, it has directed attention to the
need for establishing professional curricula in universities and colleges providing for the specific training of men and women for
entry into this branch of the public service. This important development is considered in some detail in Chapter II.

Aptitudes. Exceptional personal qualities are necessary for
the satisfactory performance of police duty. Many of them are
quite fundamental and should be present to a degree beyond that
of the average individual. Among the qualities which have proved
especially significant are the following:

Initiative	Tactfulness
Alertness	Forcefulness
Observation **power**	Self-reliance
Ideation	Speed of movement
Speed of thought	Economic intelligence
Self-confidence	Ability to work under **distraction**
Self-assertion	Accuracy of thought
Freedom from gullibility	Organizing ability
Visual memory	Flexibility
Auditory memory	Cooperativeness
Physical courage	Oral Expression
Moral courage	Vocabulary
Judgment	Written expression
Adaptability	Discretion
Curiosity	Discrimination
Imagination	Diligence
Resourcefulness	Ability to follow directions
Reasoning power	Vigor
Power of concentration	Wide range of interests
Persistence	Wide range of information
Endurance	Assembling ability
Perception	Arithmetical reasoning
Energy	Mathematical capacity
Patience	Social intelligence.

---

⁴Vollmer, August: *The Police and Modern Society,* University of California Press,
1936, p. 222.
See footnote 1, Chapter II, for sources of aptitude tests.

Vollmer stated the situation accurately when he said that the average citizen expects the police officer "to have the wisdom of Solomon, the courage of David, the strength of Samson, the patience of Job, the leadership of Moses, the kindness of the Good Samaritan, the strategy of Alexander, the faith of Danied, the diplomacy of Lincoln, the tolerance of the Carpenter of Nazareth, and finally, an intimate knowledge of every branch of the natural, biological and social sciences."[4]

Character. The character and reputation of a police officer must be unassailable. Police entrance examination procedure includes the taking of three sets of fingerprints from the candidate. One is retained for the departmental files, one is forwarded to the State Bureau of Criminal Records and Identification, and the third to the Federal Bureau of Investigation in Washington, D. C. This is a highly important phase of the recruiting process, since police departments—first of all—must assure themselves that they are not employing persons with criminal records.

In addition, inquiry is made of persons mentioned as references in the candidate's application form. It should be noted that references, as such, given by the applicant constitute the weakest source of information concerning his character and that the greatest reliance should be placed upon other channels of investigation. A detailed report should be secured from the police department in the applicant's home town if he has resided elsewhere. These measures will uncover important information concerning the candidate's relations with friends and previous employers, his credit standing, and his reputation with persons qualified to judge his integrity and reliability.

All inquiries should be conducted by capable investigators and every effort expended to obtain all the information possible concerning the applicant's life history and habits. An inspection of the application form shown in Appendix A will indicate the wide range of investigative leads furnished by the application itself. This stage of the screening process should be considered as qualifying only and there should be no hesitation in rejecting applicants whose previous reputation for character is not of the highest type. All borderline cases should be resolved against the applicant and in favor of the department.

The Residence Requirement. A disabling obstacle to career service in the police field is the "home talent" tradition in American cities and communities. This expresses itself in the local residence requirement for appointment to the force. A 1961 survey by the International Association of Chiefs of Police revealed that nearly 75 percent of the responding departments had pre-service residency requirements, varying from six months to five years. Since nearly all police departments are experiencing difficulty in filling positions up to authorized strength, these restrictions interfere seriously with attempts to improve the quality of police personnel.

The local residence requirement denies the police and the community they serve the opportunity to recruit promising candidates who may, in some instances, provide a superior grade of qualifications that may be lacking among local applicants. The police and local officials in the community should immediately take steps to abolish the local resident requirement and should also encourage the removal of state residency requirements, if they exist.

Every effort should be made to overcome the pernicious requirement of local residence and replace it with a more enlightened policy that would be in the public interest. It is noteworthy that in recent years, an increasing number of cities and communities have abandoned the residence qualification and require only that the candidate be a citizen of the United States.

Once police entrance standards are established and a list of applicants is available, the next important step is the mechanism of selection.

II

THE MECHANICS OF SELECTION
The Search for Candidates

Following the establishment of adequate entrance standards, the next and perhaps the most essential phase of the whole recruitment process is an active search for qualified candidates. The best selection procedure that can be devised will be ineffective if not applied to the most outstanding group of men that can be attracted to the examination. A thorough canvass should be made of all likely sources of candidates. Appropriate publicity concerning forthcoming police entrance examinations can be planned and executed with telling effect. Where the residence requirement has been disposed of, this can cover a comparatively wide area.

There is a certain fascination in police work that is characteristic of no other profession and which can prove useful in attracting candidates. Men in all walks of life are intrigued by the detective mystery thriller, detective feature series on television and front-page stories of major crimes, despite the fact that all of these present for the most part an inadequate image of police service.

Any police officer will certify that these presentations, dramatized againt a backdrop of murder and graft for the benefit of the gullible reader or listener, are seldom in agreement with the facts and fail to portray the challenging dimensions of police service in a modern social order. Police operations are infinitely more interesting than the year's best mystery thriller. Nevertheless, this widespread popular interest in crime and the criminal has not yet been exploited to any impressive advantage in the recruiting process.

Coordinating Recruiting. Police departments and police associations in each state should take the initiative and pool their resources in the establishment of a coordinated statewide recruiting program. This would be especially helpful to the smaller departments, where the field of potential candidates is limited. A coordinated statewide recruiting program offers the following advantages:

17

1. It makes possible a more widespread recruiting effort.
2. More sophisticated advertising of openings is justified.
3. In the smaller department, it provides the opportunity to conduct recruiting and selection programs under the leadership of professional personnel officers.
4. The applicant has the opportunity of taking a single examination for openings in several jurisdictions.
5. Potential candidates would be informed of all vacancies in police departments throughout the state.
6. More extensive budgets could be appropriated for recruiting at substantially less cost than would be necessarily incurred by individual departments.
7. Uniform procedures in applying for positions in all departments could be formulated.

In those states where Commissions on Police Selection and Training Standards* have been established, the Commission is in an excellent position to organize and administer a coordinated statewide recruiting program.

An effort should be made to attract the most able young men obtainable, which means that police service enters a highly competitive market in the search for talent and ability. Needless to say, this involves the establishment of a salary structure that will enable this branch of the public service to compete with business and industry in attracting to police service high grade personnel.

The average taxpayer should be delighted to learn that this can be done without any extraordinary increase in the expenditure of public funds. It has been demonstrated that with a higher order of human material, fewer men can do a better job in less time, thus releasing budget funds *for salary* adjustments. The police salary structure is considered in greater detail later in this chapter.

The Preliminary Interview

Interested applicants should be required to present themselves at the office of the chief of police for a preliminary personal interview. It is possible at this time to screen out those who, for one reason or another are obviously not suited for police work. Badly impaired vision, nervous spasms, physical defects, gross mannerisms and other such disqualifying characteristics can be detected empir-

*See Chapter III.

ically without difficulty, and they should remove the candidate immediately from further consideration. If the applicant passes inspection during the preliminary interview, he is provided with a personal history questionnaire and application form.[5]

The Audit of Applications

A perusal of the application form and personal history questionnaire will reveal the tremendous amount of information that the applicant is compelled to give concerning himself. None of these items are unimportant or ambiguous. Each one has a specific and well-defined purpose.

Those individuals whose applications clearly indicate that they do not meet the entrance requirements should be rejected at once and notified to that effect. There would be no purpose in loading examination procedure with individuals who can be eliminated on the basis of other disqualifying information. As indicated previously, it should be noted that the usefulness of the Application Form does not end at this point. It also provides leads for the later investigation of the applicant's character and reputation.

The personal history questionnaire and application form, together with examination papers and examination scores, are subsequently filed in the Applicant's personnel folder for future reference.

The Written Examination

Basic to the screening process is the written examination. All applicants who meet the minimum standards set by the department, as indicated by the oral interview and their application forms, are admitted to the entrance examination. This is a crucial point in police selection procedure.

The means for improving selective methods in police personnel procedure are now ready at hand.[6] With the employment of care-

---

[5]See Appendix B for typical announcement of police entrance examination, personal history questionnaire and application form.

---

[6]Information concerning personnel tests and testing materials may be obtained from World Book Company, Yonkers-on Hudson 5, New York, N. Y.; Bureau of Educational Measurements, Kansas State Teachers College, Emporia, Kansas; Educational Test Bureau, 720 Washington Avenue, S. E., Minneapolis, Minnesota; and the U. S. Civil Service Commission, Washington, D. C.

fully validated and standardized tests there is as much difference between selection on the basis of their results and haphazard selection as between the purchase of an automobile "sight unseen" and its purchase after careful trial.

The intelligent use of tests and examinations, now accepted as standard procedure in the best American police departments, will go far toward reducing the element of chance in the selection of police personnel. Contact with the police personnel officer in nearby cities and the state police will prove very fruitful in connection with the content of the written examination. It should include at least one recognized intelligence test, such as the Army Alpha, the Otis Self-Administering Test, and the Henmon-Nelson Test of Mental Ability.

All of the foregoing suggestions enumerated in this chapter, and those to follow, apply with particular force to the smaller departments where the successful delivery of police service rests upon the shoulders of a comparatively few men.

The Psychiatric Screening of Police Applicants

Any written examination has both its usefulness and its limitations. It may not expose the neurotic individual who becomes irritable and brings the department into disrepute by his actions and who is frequently the subject of disciplinary action. Because of poor coordination he is often injured either on or off duty. The mentally or emotionally unstable person may take life unnecessarily, become brutal and commit other abnormal acts which may subject the department and the city to damage suits and other forms of embarrassment. The temperamental individual makes trouble in the ranks and among the citizens. He is destructive of both morale and public relations, and must be eventually replaced.

The emotional stability to withstand the stresses of police work must, of necessity, be a primary requisite of police personnel. Officers must rationally cope with violence, verbal abuse, resentment and emergencies. The emotionally unfit cannot meet these stresses. One incompetent officer can trigger a riot, permanently damage the reputation of a citizen, or alienate the community against a police department. Police service operates within a context of danger and emergency, and the emotionally unstable person is no match for the exacting demands police duty will impose upon him.

Although a comprehensive character investigation may eliminate some socially maladjusted individuals, personality defects in some of the applicants will be latent and not easily discernible. Hence, the necessity for psychiatric screening in order to protect the department against the danger of moving an acute personality problem into the ranks. Its extreme usefulness as a screening tool in exposing those personal traits which are incompatible with service in a police uniform have been amply demonstrated. The experience of the Los Angeles Police Department is most convincing in this respect. Dr. James H. Rankin, psychiatrist for that department, stated:[7]

> In the Los Angeles Police Department, in one year, there were four thousand two hundred thirty-nine person who filed for the entrance examination. Of this group, one thousand nine hundred eighty-nine passed the written Civil Service examination, approximately forty-seven percent. Of this number, one thousand two hundred ninety-two passed the Physical Agility Test. Of this remaining group, only six hundred twenty-nine passed the oral examination, less than fifteen percent of those who originally filed. By the time the medical examinations were completed, there were only one hundred eighty-eight persons still surviving.
>
> Of these, one hundred sixty-one took the psychiatric examination. Of this small group, twenty-five failed, or 15.6 percent. One hundred nineteen men went into the Police Academy for thirteen weeks of basic training. Of this number, only one hundred and three men put on uniforms and went to work "in the field" out of four thousand two hundred thirty-nine who filed for the examination, a percentage of 2.4!

What those twenty-five men could contribute in terms of damage to one of the nation's finest police departments, challenges the imagination. Dr. Rankin's statement points up not only the yield from psychiatric screening but the critical importance of the total police entrance examination—out of a total of four thousand two hundred thirty-nine applicants who originally filed for the examination, four thousand one hundred thirty-six failed and were weeded out at the intake as unfit for police service!

---

[7]Rankin, James H., M.D., Preventive Psychiatry in the Los Angeles Police Department, *Police*, Thomas, Vol. 1, No. 6, July-August 1957, pp. 24-29.

Collateral Elements of the Police Recruiting Process

The Qualifying Oral Interview. The oral interview is the final stage in the initial recruitment process. The interview should be conducted by the chief of police in such a manner as to appraise the traits of personal appearance, ability to meet others, social intelligence, ability of the candidate to express himself and his apparent ability to fit into the departmental organization. Generally speaking, this interview may aid in determining likeableness, affability, attitude toward work, outside interests, forcefulness, conversational ability and disagreeable mannerisms. The score on the total entrance examination is computed for qualifying candidates and they are ranked on the eligibility list in the order of their final grades. Since selection is based upon merit, the applicant with the highest score is qualified for the first vacancy in his position classification.

The foregoing selection procedure will produce the best possible police recruits, but no recruiting process is so perfect that it will not occasionally pass candidates who will fail when tested by the actual performance of police duties. There are men of intelligence, character and ability who never, under any circumstances, can become good police officers; they may work hard, long, loyally and faithfully and yet prove incompetent. In the interest of the service as well as for their own good, such men should be eliminated at an early date.

The Probationary Period. A probationary period is thus an indispensable part of the examination process. A probationary period of not less than one year, preferably two, is recommended during which superior officers may give close attention to the candidate's actual ability to do police work before tenure protection becomes absolute.

There are many undesirable traits that can be and will be kept under control by the new recruit for short periods of time. Even a periodic drunk might not be discovered, or an epileptic escape notice. The lazy person would naturally speed up while he was without tenure protection and the temperamental person would be able to keep himself under control for short periods. However, it would be rare indeed, if competent supervision were provided, adequate training courses established, frequent ratings taken and work performance studied over a two-year period, that the potentially unsatisfactory recruit would remain in the organization.

This check on performance is concerned with the probationer's capacity to understand and execute directions, his alertness and the rapidity with which he learns the techniques of a patrolman's job, his ability to fit into the organization harmoniously, his loyalty to the force and his skill in performing police duties. He can be dismissed without the filing of charges and without a hearing at any time during probation.

It is quite natural for a probationer to put his best foot forward and to cooperate in every way with the police training program, which should be more or less continuous during this period. He will in the majority of cases attempt to conform to the rules for conduct, matters of policy, and standards of quantity and quality of work performed. If the period is sufficiently long, the probationer will form habits which are in agreement with departmental standards and which he will not be likely to abandon in the future.

No probationer should be given tenure until the end of the probationary period and only upon the specific recommendation of his superiors. Occasionally, rank and tenure are acquired by default. The only safe practice is to drop summarily all probationers who do not demonstrate something above minimum ability and performance on the job, for once given rank, it is more difficult to eliminate incompetents. The department should be given the benefit of the doubt in all borderline cases.

The Rating of Police Personnel. Some form of rating system by which superior officers may at regular intervals appraise the desirable and undesirable qualities of the new recruit, is a necessary and important phase of police personnel management.

Why have rating systems? For the following reasons:
1. For the same reason that we have examinations to determine the applicant's degree of intelligence and adaptability.
2. To determine his efficiency on the job.
3. To assist him in increasing his efficiency and, thereby, the efficiency of the organization.

4. As a basis for determining his fitness for promotion or salary increase.

5. As a basis for determining what branch of the service he is best fitted for.

6. To stimulate and keep alive the personnel spirit.

7. To make supervisory officers more analytical in their judgments of men under their supervision.

8. To rate by use of the rating scheme the ability of the rater and his success in building up the efficiency of his subordinates.

9. To discover the reason why men who have previously done good work go into a slump, and to help them overcome the difficulty.

10. To eliminate probationers whom the examination failed to detect as inadaptable, or who are adaptable but who will not apply their abilities.

Although on occasion personal bias on the part of the rater may influence his judgment to some degree, a rating scale and its use is more than justified if it does the following:

Points out the highly adaptable.

Points out the leaders.

Points out the energetic workers.

Points out the drones.

Points out those with special abilities.

Points out the temperamentally unfitted.

Points out the moral tone of the individual.

Points out the defects in the organization.

Aids in morale development.

Speeds up the organization.

The sum total of:

Examination results, plus

Training school records, plus

Work load carried plus

Success in satisfactorily disposing of the load, plus

Rating scale average — equals

Efficiency records

Training, plus

Counseling, plus

Study and aiding to improve low averages in traits and performance, plus

Correction of morale, plus
Removal of factors causing the problem — equals
    Efficiency of supervised and supervisor.

Rating procedure thus becomes integrated with the probationary period as a continuing part of the screen process. Those individuals who cannot or do not measure up to departmental standards of performance need to be eliminated at as early a stage as possible.

The Police Cadet System

A relatively prosperous and expanding economy has placed the police in a serious competitive position with business and industry in recruiting personnel. Elevated entrance requirements and higher selection standards have further complicated the problem. The typical yield in recent years in terms of qualified personnel has averaged about 8 percent of the total number of applicants. It will be recalled that the yield in one typical year in the Los Angeles Police Department was 2. 4 percent. Recruiting has become a major police problem.

The problem is aggravated by the circumstance that police regulations in most jurisdictions seldom permit individuals to qualify for police work until they have attained the age of twenty-one. By the time they have reached this age, most young men have either completed all or most of their college work in another area of interest or have become well established in some other occupation.

An increasing number of American police departments are turning to the police cadet system as an important partial solution to a critical police recruiting problem.

Under this plan, the police cadet enters police service as a civilian employee immediately upon graduation from high school, usually at the age of eighteen. They are selected through the regular competitive police entrance examination. Requirements relating to character, intelligence, emotional stability, aptitude, height, weight, vision, strength, agility and general health are identical with those required by the department for its regular patrolmen. Upon attaining the age of twenty-one, the cadet is promoted to the rank of patrolman and becomes a uniformed police officer.

Cadets are usually assigned to the performance of clerical duties and generally are rotated to the various units of the department in order to observe and learn police methods and procedures. They have no police powers. In addition to their work assignments, they are required to attend departmental training schools and in some instances, they may be encouraged or required to work toward a university or college degree in the police science major. As a general rule, the cadet's maximum salary averages about 75 per cent of the average maximum salary of patrolmen and ranges from $250.00 per month to a maximum high of $400.00 per month in one department.

The advantages of the police cadet system appear to be clearly well established. First of all, it provides the police with a new and added recruiting mechanism, reaching young men before their interest in other vocational areas has become well developed. The period from eighteen to twenty-one is regarded as probationary in character and affords the department an excellent opportunity to observe and evaluate the cadet's performance on the job.

In addition, by the time he is appointed as a patrolman, the cadet has already had the advantage of extensive police training. From the standpoint of the individual cadet, he is provided with an immediate job opportunity on graduation from high school. Supplementing these advantages, he is given the chance to develop and cultivate an interest in police service as a career and to develop the attitudes and outlook essential to successful performance as a professional police officer.

The police cadet system is now operating in the following jurisdictions, among others: Alabama State Police, Baltimore County Police; and in the police departments of New York City, N. Y.; Cincinnati, Ohio; Detroit, Michigan; Fresno, California; Hamilton, Ontario, Toronto, Ontario; Honolulu, Hawaii; Milwaukee, Wisconsin; Philadelphia, Pennsylvania; Rockford, Illinois; San Diego, California; Seattle, Washington; Aiken, South Carolina; and Berkeley, California.

It would appear that the police cadet system is particularly well adapted to the needs of the smaller department. In the smaller community where the field of selection is limited, it would provide the department with a new and additional source of candidates for the force. In addition, the police cadet system offers to the smaller department all of the advantages it gives to the police in the larger cities, including the following:

1. An added recruiting mechanism.
2. Contacts promising young men before they have developed an interest in other occupational areas.
3. Gives the high-school graduate an immediate job opportunity.
4. The young man has the advantage of extensive police training before reaching the age of twenty-one years.
5. The fourth item is of equal value to the department.
6. Opportunity to develop career attitudes and outlook.
7. Provides the department with an excellent opportunity to observe and evaluate the young man.
8. The cadet assumes clerical and related duties, releasing personnel for other assignments.

Personnel Records

A single file folder should be maintained for each officer in the department which would include the following:

1. Personal history questionnaire and application form.
2. Results of character investigation.
3. Scores made on all phases of the entrance examination, together with examination papers.
4. Record during probation.
5. Scores made on rating scales.
6. Results of training school examinations.
7. Performance record on duty, including such matters as percentage of cases cleared, etc.
8. Letters of commendation received concerning the officer.
9. Citations for distinguished service in line of duty.
10. Record of all disciplinary measures addressed to the officer, including reprimands, warnings, suspensions, dismissal, etc.

11. Telegrams, letters and other communications received concerning the officer.
12. Record of equipment issued to the officer.
13. All other information which combined together in one file will furnish a complete personnel biography of the individual officer.

The value of a well-ordered personnel records system to the chief of police is not to be underestimated. During promotional examinations, as well as on all other occasions where the personnel factor is involved, it is indispensable.

The Police Salary Structure

It has been previously emphasized that the character and calibre of police service for years to come are determined largely by recruiting standards at the intake today. This is the fact of life and it carries with it important implications in terms of the police salary structure.

The technical nature of every phase of police service is such that police administrators must be in a position to compete with business and industry for the best human material. This means very simply and very directly that the police salary structure must be competitive. It must be sufficiently high to attract candidates to the examination room who are qualified to meet the exacting demands of police service in a modern social order. This applies with convincing force to the police in the smaller communities where such a large segment of police service is delivered in this country.

In recent years, police salary structures have moved generally upward. In sixteen typical American cities, the average starting salary for a patrolman was $564 per month in the late 1960's. The average salary after three years of service was $658 per month. Police salaries are higher in those departments noted for their professional standards of performance. In cities along the Pacific Coast, police salaries have increased more than in other sections of the country. However, the trend toward improved compensation is clearly observable throughout the United States.

It is something of an anomaly, however, that police personnel in the smaller departments have not shared too well in this trend toward improved salary structures. In view of the volume of police service accounted for in the more than 33,000 smaller communities of this country, the situation is hardly a commendable one and it is not consistent with the nature of police duties and responsibilities.

One of the difficulties in the past and in the present has been a widespread tendency to handcuff police salaries to salary levels prevailing in fire departments. This unfortunate combination is based upon the illusion that police and fire protection are of much the same nature.

Superficially, there may be some resemblance. Both police officers and firemen are engaged in the protection of life and property. But there the analogy ends. The day-to-day problems of the two departments have litttle in common. The police deal almost wholly with human relations while the work of the fireman is largely related to physical property.

Fosdick summed up the situation in these words as early as 1921:[8]

> The problems of fire extinguishment are physically definable and the work of fire prevention is highly specialized and easily reduced to mechanical standards; the uniformed force of the fire department deals with material elements. The police force deals largely with human relations; its problems are to a certain extent intangible. Firemen work in groups under the immediate direction of their superior officers; they respond to a fire in their properly assigned places and employ chemicals and other equipment as they are ordered by their officers in charge. The policeman's work is done largely on his own initiative, prompted by his own judgment.
>
> Policies affecting fire administration relate almost entirely to the financial aspects of providing men and equipment that are necessary in the light of definitely known insurance rates and fire hazards. Policies of police administration involve social and moral needs which are far removed from such factors as the storage of inflammables, hose and water pressure and building regulations.
>
> There is no divided opinion about the desirability of putting out fires; there is considerable room for the division of opinion as to how much money the city should pay for the intangible returns of crime prevention

---

[8]Fosdick, Raymond B.: *Police Administration,* Cleveland Foundation Survey of Criminal Justice in Cleveland, 1921, p. 15.

to be achieved through an enlarged and better equipped police force, or even as to how far the police should go in curbing individual liberties in their efforts to prevent crime. Thus, although these two forces are similarly organized, the objectives of their work are found to be wholly different and their methods of procedure widely dissimilar, while the values of their work are appraised on entirely different bases.

It is undoubtedly true that this linkage of police and fire compensation has embarrassed the development of police administration in the United States. Based upon a comparison of the duties and responsibilities of the two services, one comes to the conclusion that personnel resources equal to the complex demands of modern police service are unobtainable at the salary levels prevailing in fire departments.

Fosdick's suggestions concerning the differences in the functions and responsibilities in the two areas clearly indicates the inequity of any attempt to associate these two branches of the public service within the same salary structure. As professionalization of the police proceeds and the means for measurement of municipal activities are perfected, the professional distance between the two services may be expected to increase.

The foregoing considerations have important implications for the police in the smaller communities of the nation. The mobility of the criminal population today means simply that the exposure of the smaller community to criminal attack has increased on a disturbing scale. This, together with the growing complexity of the traffic problem, place a high premium on the quality of police personnel and police performance in these communities.

The officials of local government would do well to reexamine their thinking in this respect with the view of adjusting police salaries upward to the point where they will be consistent with the quality and quantity of work to be done. Mounting crime rates, together with the growing demands of traffic control, are grounds for sober reflection on the part of these officials. They are under obligation to the community and its security to see to it as the first order of business that the personnel resources of the police are equal to the urgent needs of our time.

III

POLICE TRAINING

Even after police recruits are selected by the best methods available, the police structure will continue to remain unsound as long as it is generally assumed that a person with any type of training or with none at all, is qualified to perform police duties. An in-service police training facility, staffed by the most competent officers available and operating continuously the year around, must be made available to every police officer in every department.

This is especially true in view of the fact that the police recruit must, for some time to come, be accepted in the raw, unprepared for the rigorous and exacting responsibilities of police service. Unlike workers in health, engineering and the other professions, he must be trained on the job at public expense.

In-service training has found expression in the American police services in a wide variety of forms. Until about 1915, the accepted concept that there is "more law in the end of a nightstick than in all the law books", was the operating criterion of the police officer. Any idea that a policeman should "go to school" would have been received with both astonishment and skepticism.

Preparation for police service, like that in other professional fields, had its beginnings in a form of apprenticeship. Without previous training of any kind whatsoever, the new recruit was instructed to don a uniform and a gun and go to work. As a freshman in the school of experience, he began to learn what he could at public expense through a process of trial and error, with the errors predominating. Personal instruction began when it became the practice to send the new recruit out with an experienced police officer. This procedure adapted itself quite well to the prevailing system of double officer patrol.

In 1931, the Wickersham Commission found in a survey of 383 cities that only 20 percent conducted police training schools for the new recruit. In the majority of cities surveyed, particularly the smaller cities, there was not even a pretext of training. In the counties, and smaller towns and villages, the Commission reported that the assumption of badge, revolver and the authority of law, had no prerequisite whatsoever, in terms of police training and police experience.[1]

Information is lacking concerning the first appearance in this country of formal recruit training. There are grounds for believing that instruction in the care and use of firearms ushered in the idea of police training for the new recruit. The instructional program gradually expanded to include a limited amount of criminal law, the content of city ordinances, the basic principles of criminal investigation and the departmental rules and regulations.

A number of enterprising police chiefs were impressed with the results of the training efforts and police budgets began to include some provision for formal in-service training programs. By 1935, well-organized and well-equipped in-servcie training schools were functioning in the police departments of Wichita, Indianapolis, Cincinnati, Chicago, Berkeley, Louisville, San Francisco, New York City and a number of other cities. The course content of in-service recruit training programs continued to expand until today, it reflects in an impressive degree the dimensions and problems of modern police service.

Inspired by the Federal Bureau of Investigation, which dramatized the need, set standards and provided curricula and instructors, the police have made significant strides during the past thirty years in the widespread development of formal recruit training programs. In 1965, a survey of 1,352 cities conducted by the International City Managers Association, found that 1,135 police departments were operating some type of recruit training programs for their officers.

A recent survey of 269 police departments by the National League of Cities, conducted in 1966, reported that 97 percent of the departments surveyed were engaged in formal police recruit training. But another survey of 4,000 police departments in 1965

---

[1]National Commission on Law Observance and Enforcement, *Report on the Police* (U. S. Government Printing Office), 1931, p. 19.

by the International Association of Chiefs of Police revealed that 85 percent of the officers appointed were sent into the field prior to their recruit training.[2]

It is now generally conceded that in-service police training should find expression at five different levels:

1. Recruit training (required of all new appointees).
2. Refresher training (required of all officers below the rank of Sergeant).
3. Unit training—preparation for assignment to any one of the following staff and line units—patrol, detective, records, crime prevention, vice and traffic.
4. Supervisory and command officers.
5. Administrative officers.

Recruit Training. It is essential that all new appointees to the department be exposed to the recruit training program. The course content of this program is a matter of the greatest importance. It is now widely accepted that the following course subjects should be included in the recruit training school:

Required Courses

1. Classroom notetaking.
2. The role of law enforcement.
3. Police-community relations.
4. Police ethics.
5. Racial and minority groups.
6. Laws of arrest, search and Seizure, Constitutional guarantees.
7. Code of criminal procedure, criminal law.
8. Vehicle and traffic law.
9. Traffic control.
10. Traffic accident investigation.
11. Laws of evidence.

---

[2]The President's Commission on Law Enforcement and the Administration of Justice, *Task Force Report, the Police* (U. S. Government Printing Office), 1967, p. 138.

12. Evidence resources in a criminal case, including the crime scene search.
13. Collection, care, identification and preservation of evidence.
14. Court organization and procedure.
15. Courtroom demeanor and testifying.
16. Basic criminal investigation.
17. Notetaking and report writing.
18. Interviews, interrogation, Admissions, Statements.
19. The patrol function.
20. Care and use of firearms.
21. Defensive tactics.
22. Techniques and Mechanics of arrest.
23. Emergency aid to persons.
24. Recognition and handling of abnormal persons.
25. Juvenile offender laws, juvenile court, handling of juveniles.
26. Field notetaking and crime scene recording.
27. Crowd and riot control.
28. Use of police radio and teletype.

Elective Courses

1. Investigative techniques—gambling, narcotics, prostitution.
2. Driver training.
3. Care and maintenance of police equipment.
4. Administration of criminal justice.
5. Fingerprint identification
6. Jail procedures.
7. Jurisdiction of other law enforcement agencies.
8. Police records system.
9. Powers and duties of the sheriff.
10. Raid techniques, stake-outs, surveillance.
11. Scientific aids (the crime laboratory).
12. Police-press relations.
13. Transportation of prisoners.

The facilities are potentially available for an effective police-training program in this country and the police field itself is in general agreement concerning the curriculum of an in-service training program. The problem is how to organize it and bring it to the doorstep of those who need the training.

This is particularly true of the smaller departments where, in many instances, it would be impractical to organize and put into operation an in-service police training school. Authorities agree that it would be economically feasible to establish a departmental training school where the personnel strength was fifteen to twenty, or more, and that it would not be feasible to do so with groups of two or three officers.

The answers appear to be coming into focus and at an accelerated tempo during the past two decades. Over the years, metropolitan police departments have on occasion extended their training facilities to members of the smaller police forces in surrounding suburban areas. Under this arrangement, a few selected officers attended the metropolitan school from communities within a radius of from fifty to one hundred miles. A centralized school where police personnel in a given area were exposed to the same pattern of instruction was an important step forward. Thus, in addition to other advantages, it served the purpose of promoting coordination in blockades and other operations which involve large scale cooperation over an extended area in the emergency.

Regional In-Service Training Schools

The almost total lack of any departmental training program in the smaller communities and the failure of some larger departments to inaugurate adequate training programs suggested the organization of in-servic police training schools on a regional basis.

The Federal Bureau of Investigation has for a number of years placed at the disposal of local law enforcement agencies the superb training facilities of that organization. Under the name of the National Police Academy, this program is available to selected officers from police departments in every part of the United States. The objective of this school is to train selected men of special ability and promise as instructors, so that they may return to their respective organizations and impart the training they received to their associates. The Federal Bureau of Investigation has also conducted a series of regional law enforcement conferences in all of the states, which are in the nature of short training schools for police personnel. Such schools are usually scheduled at central points and officers attend them from the surrounding area.

Some state police organizations have also made their training facilities available to local law enforcement agencies through the staging of regional training schools. The resources of the state have also been applied to police in-service training through other channels. Texas Agricultural and Mechanical College, Pennsylvania State College, Iowa State College, Uivnersity of Oklahoma, Michigan State College, Indiana University and other educational institutions have made notable contributions in the organization of in-service training programs on a zone or regional basis.

In the state of Washington, the University of Washington, Washington State University, the Washington State Patrol and the State Board for Vocational Training pooled their resources toward the organization and administration of a state-wide training program designed to reach every police officer in the state. The program contemplated a central training school for new police recruits, a series of zone schools scheduled to blanket the state, a school for specialists, a school for supervisory and command personnel, administrators' conferences and other related activities. But a change in administration at the University of Washington brought all of these beautiful plans to an inglorious end. A faculty committee took over the reins of adminstration at that institution in the interim pending the selection of a new President. One of the policies adopted by the committee was to abolish activities of the university that were not strictly academic in nature, in order to divert budget funds into salary increases for the faculty! The projected police training program was one of the casualties. But, there was good news for police training in the offing.

A New Era

The American police service has now entered a new era in terms of its most vital resource—personnel. Escaping the attention of most observers, the time is now close at hand when the best in police practice and procedure will be brought to the doorstep of every police officer in the nation.

The new era finds expression on two major fronts—legislation at the state level prescribing minimum selection and training standards for entry into police service, and the emergence of professional police training curricula in the universities and colleges of this country. Both developments sharpen the focus on the American police field as a career service.

Minimum Selection and Training Standards. In recent years, very significant trends have appeared on the scene, marked by the passage of legislation at the state level establishing minimum selection and training standards for entry into police service.

The New York State Legislature in 1959 enacted into law the *Municipal Police Training Council Act,* which established a Council to formulate and put into operation a mandatory municipal police training program.[3] Eight police officials with extensive administrative experience were appointed by Governor Nelson A. Rockefeller to the State's Municipal Police Training Council as an advisory and policy-making body.

The Council, after the necessary study and research, adopted an eighty-hour minimum basic training course consisting of seventeen separate course subjects. Thereafter, as specified in the *Municipal Police Training Council Act,* all police officers appointed from the date of July 1, 1960, would be required to satisfactorily complete the basic course as a condition for permanent employment. The first year of operation saw the completion of thirty-five basic schools of instruction throughout the state and the awarding of certificates to 822 municipal police officers.

It is significant that these 822 graduates are employed by 267 different municipalities within the state, indicating that the benefits of this police training program have been broadly dispersed throughout every area of New York State.

At least one school was held in each of the twelve training zones outside of New York City during the first year of operation, thus

---

[3]See Appendix C, *The New York Municipal Police Training Council Act.*

making the basic training course available to new police recruits everywhere in the state. It will be noted that the minimum police training standards program in New York is mandatory. In other words, an applicant must complete satisfactorily a basic police training course before he can enter police service. It is *mandated* police training by State mandate.

As of October 23, 1960, legislation passed by the California State Legislature under the title, *Law Enforcement Standards Training Act,* went into effect.[4] The Act establishes minimum police training standards for California peace officers and provides for the certification of schools where this training may be obtained. The program is not mandatory; it is organized on a voluntary basis.

The governing Commission on Peace Officer Standards and Training allocates to cities and counties which voluntarily agree to adhere to the Commission's standards for employment and training, money from the Peace Officers Training Fund. This allocation covers one-half of the salaries of police officers who participate in this training program, in addition to certain living expenses.

It is significant to note that the individual applicant may substitute for the prescribed basic training course, satisfactory completion of a minimum of sixty credit hours in an undergraduate police science major leading to a degree at any university or college certified by the Commission.

Today, in California, police training that meets the standards of the Commission is statewide; it blankets the state and exceeds by far any to be found elsewhere in the nation, with the exception of the state of New York. In California by 1966, 98 percent of the population in that state was being served by police departments which adhered to the prescribed minimum standards for police training.[5]

As of June 3, 1961, state legislation became effective in New

---

[4]See Appendix D, *California Law Enforcement Standards and Training Act.*

---

[5]The President's Commission on Law Enforcement and Administration of Justice, *Task Force Report: The Police,* 1967, p. 217.

Jersey, prescribing minimum training standards for entry into police service. The training is undertaken during the probationary period of one year and prior to permanent appointment as a police officer. The program is organized on a voluntary basis.[6]

Similarly, in Oregon, state legislation was passed, effective June 1, 1961, creating an Advisory Board on Police Standards and Training.[7] The Act recommends minimum physical, emotional, intellectual and moral standards and minimum police training standards.

Here again, the participation of police departments in the program is on a voluntary basis. However, the Board received in a comparatively short time favorable responses from half the police departments in the state, indicating they either (1) already had in effect standards equivalent to or higher than the minimum requirements recommended by the Board, or (2) highly favor the recommendations of the Board and will make every effort to voluntarily comply.

By 1969, legislation at the state level prescribing minimum police selection and training standards had been enacted in nine states. In a number of other states, similar legislation is under consideration. It is now apparent that this development in the American police field marks a new milestone in police in-service training.

Apparently, it is just a matter of time until every state in the nation will have established minimum standards for the selection and training of police officers. This means that police best practice and procedure in the training of police personnel is on the way toward making total contact with the field, including especially the smaller police departments of this country.

As an important step in this direction, in 1966, a Model Police Standards Council Act was drafted by the Advisory Council on Police Training and Education, and the Professional Standards

---

[6]See Appendix E, *The New Jersey Act Relating to Training of Policemen prior to Permanent Appointment.*

[7]See Appendix F, *The Oregon Act: Police Standards and Training.*

Division of the International Association of Chiefs of Police.[8] It offers to the states a legislative model or pattern which can be followed in the establishment of minimum standards for the selection and training of police personnel.

Police departments and state police associations in those states where such enabling legislation has not yet been passed should make strong and effective contact with the members of their legislatures and call their attention to these developments. Such action will accelerate the day when police personnel in all of the smaller police departments of the nation will have the benefit of adequate police selection and training facilities.

It should be emphasized at this point that the recruit training period is an integral part of the entrance examination process. The recruit is on probation during this time and he may be "screened out" if he fails to meet the standards of the department in any way. The recruit training period provides an excellent opportunity to uncover disqualifying characteristics that escaped detection during previous stages of the examination.

The reasons for elimination at this point are as numerous as there are individuals. Domestic discord in the home, dishonesty, insubordination, infidelity, lack of interest and enthusiasm for the job, temperamental defects, drinking, lack of punctuality, inability to get along with associates, poor attention to personal appearance, and inadequate response to training, are typical of traits whose degree and permanence are difficult to measure on conventional entrance examination tests. However, it would be virtually impossible for the recruit to conceal these defects for a period of one year, while working under pressure and under the close scrutiny and observation of superior officers.

The foregoing comments have been concerned primarily with the development of police recruit training schools. The same state-sponsored facilities can also be addressed to refresher training, and the training of supervisory and command personnel and administrative officers.[9]

---

[8]See Appendix G, *Model Police Standards Council Act Drafted by the International Association of Chiefs of Police.*

Refresher training. All officers below the rank of Sergeant should be given refresher training at periodical intervals. In addition to a review of selected areas covered in the recruit training program, it serves the purpose of keeping officers abreast of the times. New developments and innovations and new police procedures are constantly appearing on the scene. The refresher training program provides an excellent opportunity for keeping personnel informed concerning these developments.

Unit Training. Ideally, upon assignment to a unit or division or bureau in the organization, the officer should have the benefit of some preparation geared to the work to be performed. Thus, workers in the police records unit are confronted with tasks that are altogether different from those in other areas of the organization. The necessity for specialized training is equally apparent upon assignment to patrol service. The situation is the same when the officer is assigned to traffic, crime prevention, communications, detective and vice operations.

Supervisory and Command Officers. For in-service training purposes, supervisory and comand officers include sergeants, lieutenants and captains, or ranks below that of administrative officers. Instruction of supervisory and command personnel should be conducted by the conference method as distinguished from the classroom approach in recruit training. The content of the instructional program should be based upon the elements of leadership, supervision and command. Army manuals will prove invaluable in this phase of the training program. Available instructors should be supplemented by the appearance at these conferences of supervisory and command officers from the U. S. Army. These arrangements can be easily made. Military authorities have always shown the police the highest degree of cooperation.

Administrative Officers. Training is no less important for the highest administrative officers in the department than for first-line supervisors. As in the case of supervisory and command personnel,

---

⁹Where personnel strength is large enough to justify the operation of a departmental training school, much of this training may be delivered within the framework of the organization itself.

this part of the training program can be presented by the conference method or on a consultation basis. Again, military commanding officers whose training and experience in the management of men place them in a position to counsel with the voice of authority, are especially valuable for the purpose.

Roll-call Training. This type of training is presented during the roll-call period at the beginning of a shift and just before the officers go out on duty. Roll-call training was originally developed in the Los Angeles Police Department, where the opinion is unanimous that it has proved to be an effective training device. It does not replace the rigorous program of the Los Angeles Police Training Academy. In implementing this program, the roll-call period was extended from fifteen to thirty minutes in order to set aside fifteen minutes for the daily roll-call training period.

The training or orientation is presented by supervisory and command officers. However, this does not rule out regular staff and line officers who by virtue of their special assignment, experience or qualifications, may have an important contribution to make to the program. Following are a few typical subjects presented at roll-call training which illustrate the wide range of problems that can be discussed and analyzed:

How to use the telephone.
How to use the field notebook.
How to advise citizens on crime prevention techniques.
How to testify effectively in court.
Lie detector tests and preliminary interrogation.
Care and use of firearms.
Combat shooting.
Operation of mobile radio equipment.
How to respond to a "459 There Now" call.
How to proceed with a preliminary burglary investigation.
How to answer an "ADT" alarm call.
Current criminal emergencies.
How to handle calls involving dead bodies.
How to recognize stolen vehicles.
How to work a stake-out.
How to apprehend prowlers.
How to make vagrancy arrests.
How to determine intoxication.

How to handle mentally ill persons.
Techniques in the use of tear gas.
Disaster operations.
The use of force.
Self-defense tactics.
How to preserve evidence at the scene of a crime.

Roll-call training offers to the smaller police departments an effective training device that can be used with important results in daily police operations.[10] The number of subjects that can be presented to police personnel through this method has no limit.

Teaching Methods. Whatever the form of training, qualified instructors with demonstrated teaching ability are a prerequisite. In the presentation of technical subjects, it is excellent practice to go outside to the professions and nearby universities and colleges for special instructors. The Federal Bureau of Investigation has long used civilian instructors in the National Police Academy as a part of its visiting faculty. For example, in 1966, the following civilian instructors taught in this outstanding training program: a professor of psychology, a sociologist, a chief clinical psychiatrist, four judges from various levels of the court system, a professor of history, a physicist, a chemist, a superintendent of schools, and a representative from the news media.

Most training courses are taught almost exclusively by the lecture method although professional training directors and educators recognize that this method does have some limitations. In a police training program, as in any training program, it is necessary to keep in mind some of the basic elements of the learning process.

Learning is in large part a communication of ideas from one person to another. Consequently, the senses of the learner must be brought into play. The decision on which method of instruction to use is somewhat simplified by the fact that of all the senses, sight is by far the most effective. Hence, it would appear that a pattern of presentation which combines showing and telling—the lecture-

---

[10] Under the title, *Daily Training Bulletins*, the Los Angeles Police Department has published in two volumes a complete presentation of its roll-call training program. They may be obtained from Charles C Thomas, Publisher, 301-327 East Lawrence Avenue, Springfield, Ill.

demonstration approach, takes advantage of this variation in the learning potential of the several senses of perception.

The Police Library. A first prerequisite to a police in-service training program is a good departmental library. The literature of the police field has expanded rapidly during the past quarter century. Today, reliable texts, reference works and manuals are available in every area of police operations, including police organization and management, police personnel administration, the police records system, the police communications system, criminal investigation and identification, police patrol organization, the police detective function, traffic regulation and control and police crime prevention.

It is now possible to organize and shelve a well-rounded police library with adequate texts and reference works to support a sound in-service training program. Depending on the size of the department, it may be wise to make available in the library from six to twelve copies of certain standard texts in order to meet the circulation demands of departmental personnel. Many departments follow this practice. Supplementing the departmental library, an increasing number of individual police officers are accumulating their own personal police libraries.

Police Training at the University and College Level

Today, universities and colleges are bringing their resources for training and research into contact with the personnel needs of the American police field. It is now possible for a high-school graduate to prepare for a career in police service at the university and college level in exactly the same manner as the doctor, lawyer and engineer. In any field, it goes without saying, the individual with a university background has the advantage. This is especially true in police service. In terms of professional advancement, the university graduate has a strong foundation on which to build a successful career in this branch of the public service.

As of 1969, more than 285 universities and colleges in the United States were offering academic programs in prepartion for career service in the police field, criminology and corrections. Of this number, sixty-eight were in the state of California. The following table reveals the number of institutions of higher learning in this country now offering police degree programs.

Recently, the International Association of Chiefs of Police, parent organization of the police field, with the aid of a $400,000 grant from the Ford Foundation, threw the full weight of its power and prestige behind police training at the university and college level. It can be expected with complete certainty that within a comparatively short time, university police training will blanket the nation, with a plurality of programs in every state.

As recently as 1941, there was openly expressed skepticism concerning this new development in the police training field and in the field of higher education. Today, police recruiters are on the campuses of the nation seeking out candidates for the entrance examination. Many police departments now offer extra credit on the examination where the candidate possesses a degree in the police science major. An increasing number of departments have established a minimum educational requirement of two years of college work in police science and administration. In some departments already, the candidate must present a bachelor degree in the police major in order to gain admission to the entrance examination rooms.

Based upon experience in organizing a four-year curriculum leading to the bachelor degree in police science and administration at Washington State University, the author can certify to at least one thing. The establishment of a professional curriculum in the police major at the university level is a comparatively simple academic operation.

Every university and college already includes in its offerings more than 90 percent of the subject materials that should be geared into such a professional program. Political science, public administration, sociology, psychology, biology, chemistry and physics, among others, are basic artillery pieces of the modern police officer. Today, they are considered as a necessary and essential part of his training for career service in the police field. It only remains to superimpose upon these course subjects in a four-year

Police Training

TABLE I

NUMBER OF LAW ENFORCEMENT DEGREE PROGRAMS AVAILABLE IN THE UNITED STATES AND OUTLYING AREAS

	Associate Degree Programs (2-Year)	Baccalaureate Degree Programs (4-Year)	Master's Degree Programs	Doctorate Degree Program	Number of Separate Institutions		Associate Degree Programs (2-Year)	Baccalaureate Degree Programs (4-Year)	Master's Degree Programs	Doctorate Degree Programs	Number of Separate Institutions
Alabama	2	0	0		2	Nebraska	1	1	0		1
Alaska	1	0	0		1	Nevada	2	0	0		2
Arizona	3	2	0		5	New Hampshire	0	0	0		0
Arkansas	0	0	0		0	New Jersey	3	0	0		3
California	58	6	6	2	65	New Mexico	1	1	0		1
Colorado	2	1	0		3	New York	11	1	2	2	12
Connecticut	2	1	0		2	North Carolina	2	0	0		2
Delaware	1	0	0		1	North Dakota	0	0	0		0
District of Columbia	2	1	0		2	Ohio	6	3	0		7
Florida	12	1	1	1	12	Oklahoma	0	2	0		2
Georgia	4	0	0		4	Oregon	6	2	0		8
Hawaii	1	0	0		1	Pennsylvania	7	2	0		9
Idaho	2	1	0		2	Rhode Island	1	1	0		1
Illinois	11	1	0		11	South Carolina	0	0	0		0
Indiana	1	2	0		3	South Dakota	0	0	0		0
Iowa	5	0	1		6	Tennessee	1	1	0		1
Kansas	4	0	0		4	Texas	10	1	1		10
Kentucky	1	1	0		1	Utah	2	2	0		3
Louisiana	0	1	0		1	Vermont	0	0	0		0
Maine	0	0	0		0	Virginia	4	1	0		4
Maryland	3	0	0		3	Washington	7	1	1		7
Massachusetts	3	1	0		3	West Virginia	0	0	0		0
Michigan	8	2	1		11	Wisconsin	2	1	0		3
Minnesota	0	0	0		0	Wyoming	1	0	0		1
Mississippi	0	1	0		1	Guam	1	0	0		1
Missouri	4	2	0		6	Virgin Islands	1	0	0		1
Montana	0	0	0		0		199	44	13	5	234

undergraduate program the necessary technical police subjects, following the pattern that has proven successful in the other professions. Furthermore, it has been demonstrated that this can be done within the framework of the highest existing academic standards and at negligible cost.

The extent to which the American police have become training conscious is typified by Bulletin No. 13 released by the New York City Police Department on February 24, 1969. It indicates in convincing terms the degree to which personnel in that department are now involved in training programs, both in-service and at the university level. The Bulletin stated:

New York City policemen put in more than one-third of a million student-hours of in-service advanced and specialized training during 1968, Police Commissioner Howard R. Leary disclosed today.

A total of 31,081 Patrolmen and superiors attended forty Police Department training courses conducted during the year.

In addition, the largest number of police recruits and trainees in the history of the Department took their recruit training in 1968. The Police Academy registered 3,210 Probationary Patrolmen and Policewomen and 800 Police Trainees in its 18-week recruit training program during the year.

In many respects both the in-service and recruit training programs of 1968 represented improvements and additions to courses introduced in 1967.

For both groups, recruits and veterans of the force, there was increased emphasis on human relations and community problems. All members of the force attended intensified one-day courses on these subjects at the Academy during the year to supplement their precinct unit training programs.

For recruits, training in "The Police Role in Human and Race Relations" was expanded during the year from 44 to 65 hours. This training included lectures, workshop discussions, problem-solving seminars, films, and human relations research projects. Among the areas covered were "The History of the American Negro" and "Puerto Rican Culture and Customs."

One particularly important area in which Police Department training has expanded, Commissioner Leary noted, has been in the experimental college program introduced in 1967. In that year, 35 members of a recruit class that completed its Academy training were selected to attend John Jay College of Criminal Justice (of the City University of New York) on one of the five days of their regular work week. There they took courses in the field of human relations and earned six college credits for the year's work. In 1968 the program was expanded by the addition of 21 additional Academy graduates.

The ultimate objective of this experiment is to expand the college training program to include all recruits and make it an integral part of the Department's recruit training.

Another facet of the Department's commitment to higher education was the granting of leave, with pay, to three members of the force who had won scholarships or fellowships for advanced degrees. A Sergeant is working for his Master's Degree in Criminal Justice at the state School of Criminal Justice, in Albany, under a State University of New York scholarship. Two other men are studying under fellowships provided by the Federal Office of Law Enforcement Assistance. One, a Lieutenant, is working toward a Master's Degree in Police Administration at Michigan State University. The other, a Detective, is seeking a Masters Degree in Criminology at the University of California.

During 1968, a total of 1,342 members of the force were enrolled in the John Jay College of Criminal Justice in undergraduate courses. Another 127 were enrolled in the graduate program of John Jay and six were taking graduate work at the Baruch School, another unit of the City University of New York.

In addition to training Patrolmen, the Police Academy stepped up its instructional courses for Precinct Unit Training Sergeants — the superiors responsible for in-service training of Patrolmen in their own precincts. In a 35-hour method-of-instruction course, the training Sergeants were equipped to improve the level of their on-the-job training, carried out in conjunction with the Police Academy's unit training program. This program utilizes the facilities of WNYC-TV, the city's television station.

A special command course given prior to promotion to men on the Sergeant's eligibility list, which was expanded to three weeks in 1967, was lengthened to six weeks during 1968. Major improvements in course contents and teaching methods were part of the change. Lecture time has been decreased and the prospective Sergeants are now doing more of their training in seminars, role-playing and carefully supervised field training. New areas covered include anticipatory guidance, handling the mentally ill, and special training in providing security for individuals and residential and business premises.

Another broad area in which Police Department training has been expanded is in the management development program. Particular emphasis is given to development of the student's understanding of people and his ability to communicate effectively. The career development course, essentially a study for promotion, has been expanded and special emphasis is given to the development of discretion and judgment in crisis situations.

In the area of field training, an innovation has been the establishment of practical courses in disorder control. Utilizing the facilities of the 69th Regiment Armory and unused streets and unoccupied buildings on Welfare Island, more than 5,000 Patrolmen and superiors have been trained to provide better protection for life and property in various disorder situations. In addition, all superior officers with the rank of Captain and higher have attended conferences in preparation for a series of command post exercises being carried out this year in conjunction with an operational plan for mobilizing trained precinct personnel at any hour of the day or night in disorder situations.

Other improvements and innovations in department training included the development of an orientation program for newly inducted civilian personnel and the development of a series of training brochures including guides to specialized libraries of particular interest to police researchers and of management periodicals of special interest to police administrators.

Over 1,000 detectives attended specialized courses in criminal identification and new methods of developing fingerprint evidence.

It is not difficult to perceive that in the foreseeable future, a minimum educational requirement for entry into police service will be a bachelor degree in the police science major. But, that is not all. Police administration may be expected to follow in the footsteps of the other professions in another important respect.

The lawyer, doctor, pharmacist, engineer and even the beautician and barber are required to pass a qualifying state board examination before being admitted to practice. It is interesting to note, for example, that the states began to pass legislation providing for the state board examination and licensing of barbers as early as 1893. In the early 1900's a standard text book of some 501 pages appeared for use in barber training schools which today, involve a minimum of eleven months intensive preparation.[11] Among other things, the text included orientation in the history of barbering, personal hygiene, bacteriology, anatomy, physiology, nervous and circulatory systems, and chemistry.

Surely, the work and responsibilities of a police officer and the clientele with which he deals—human beings and human personality, even life itself—are as important as a haircut! We may confidently look forward to the time when the individual will, in addition to a bachelor degree in the police major, be required to pass a qualifying state board examination before he can move into a police uniform.

---

[11]American Barber College, *Practice and Science of Standard Barbering*, 501 pp, about 1910.

University Police Training vs. In-Service Training

Police training at the university and college level reduces to a very marked degree the load on in-service training but does not take its place. Both are necessary. Each one supplements the other. The objectives of university police training are as follows:

1. To give future police officers a broad liberal arts education, in conjunction with intensive professional training for the police and other investigative services.
2. To give the future police officer a thorough command of those tools in the arts and sciences which are essential to the successful delivery of police service in a modern social order.
3. To provide a strong foundation for a career in this professional field.
4. To develop the qualities of leadership and executive potential.
5. To provide a reservoir or personnel reserve from which to draw the police chiefs of tomorrow.
6. To give a long-range perspective of the role of the police in modern society.
7. To foster the ideals of professional achievement in this branch of the public service.

On the other hand, the objectives of in-service training are more immediate in nature. They include orientation in such typical areas as the following:

1. Departmental policies.
2. Departmental rules and regulations.
3. Established police practices and procedures, vocational in nature, which are normally not included in a university police training program.
4. Development of on-the-job skills in all phases of the police operation.
5. Local police problems.
6. Refresher training.

Thus, it can be easily seen that the two training areas, although entirely different in nature and objective, are both essential to the effective delivery of police service. Both play important roles in preparing the individual officer to meet the complex demands of police service today.

It is to be observed that there is some variation in the content of the police curriculum from one institution to another. At one end of the spectrum will be found a sharp emphasis on vocational skills such as gunnery, for example. At the other end, the educational philosophy is one of training for leadership.

There is a definite movement among university police training officials to standardize curriculum content. The International Association of Chiefs of Police has expressed a strong interest in this direction. The task is made less formidable by the circumstance that approximately the same basic "core" curriculum will be found at most institutions. The problem, therefore, involves primarily a fringe operation. If a prediction could be ventured, it would indicate a reduction in the emphasis on vocational skills.

IV

SUPPORTING ELEMENTS IN PERSONNEL MANAGEMENT

Lateral Mobility of Police Personnel. The horizontal movement of personnel, particularly at the supervisory and command level, among police departments has not yet been widely accepted in the United States. However, in business and industry, lateral mobility or lateral entry is common place and has been for many years. This would appear to indicate to them that the procedure is an attractive one, both for management and personnel. The apparent advantages of this personnel mechanism for the police field invite closer scrutiny.

Promotional opportunities in the smaller police departments are somewhat limited. The number of supervisory and command positions is relatively small when compared to the total personnel strength of the department. This circumstance tends to freeze personnel in the lower ranks for extended periods of time, resulting in a possible loss of incentive and morale.

With the increasing emphasis on the police field as a career service and the growing influx of college trained personnel into the police uniform, this problem is now pressing forward for attention. The risk of frustration because of the lack of movement upward through promotional channels has important implications for police management, especially in the smaller departments.

The trend toward lateral mobility or lateral entry of police personnel is one bright light on the horizon which stands to offer an approach to this problem. For some years now, an increasing number of cities and communities have been selecting their chiefs of police through open competitive examination, not limited to members of the department concerned. It has become very common practice in Southern California, for example, for a new chief of police to be imported from some other department, and frequently from some other part of the country. A recent study indicated that at least forty California cities with populations of 10,000 or more, had selected chiefs from outside the department.

And it is increasingly the case where supervisory and command positions are being filled on an open competitive basis. Several police departments in California have recently held open competitive examinations for the rank of Captain, which were open to any law enforcement officer with the proper qualifications. These qualifications included five years of experience as a police officer plus three years as a police lieutenant, or a police sergeant with at least one year of college-level training in police science or related subjects.

Our foreign contemporaries in general support the lateral mobility concept. The British favor a plan whereby specially selected and trained officers of senior rank would be given the opportunity of seeking employment as and when vacancies occur in the senior ranks of other forces, as a promotion policy. One school of thought in high official circles is that good officer material in some of the smaller forces is often wasted because of the lack of opportunity for promotion in those forces, where the number of higher ranks in the organization is small and vacancies in them are few and far between. It is felt that appointments in the higher ranks of all police forces should be made on an open competitive basis from selected applicants recruited from forces in all parts of the country.

In a recent survey of the extent to which lateral mobility was being practiced by police departments in the United States, questionnaires were mailed to departments in 234 cities. Of the 234, 88 or 38 percent of the questionnaires were returned. The returns showed that lateral entry was being employed in ten departments. One California chief of police observed, "I believe that the lack of lateral entry is an important obstacle to professionalization in the law enforcement field.

Some of the apparent advantages of lateral mobility or entry of police personnel are as follows:

1. It opens up the channels of promotion.
2. It fosters initiative and enthusiasm for the job with the knowledge that the opportunities for advancement are greater than before.

3. It enhances police morale.
4. It encourages a career service.
5. It widens the field of candidates for supervisory, command and administrative positions in the police service.
6. Police service becomes more attractive to the police candidate and the new recruit when he knows that the channels of promotion are open and that his chances for promotion are amplified.

The Role of Women in the Smaller Department

Women were first appointed to the American police service fifty-seven years ago by the Los Angeles Police Department. This was four years before they were appointd as members of the Metropolitan Police Force of London, and seven years after the first woman was commissioned on the European continent in Stuttgart, Germany. In the early 1960's, there were 5,617 female police officers and detectives in the United States.

Anyone who enters a police headquarters building today will observe the presence of female employees, some of whom may be sworn police officers. Qualified women can prove invaluable to a police department on many types of assignments, including clerical duties, work in police staff units such as records, planning and research, front office contact with the public and on occasion, even radio dispatching.

Their services are also extremely useful in operational commands, including patrol, vice investigation, undercover assignments and other investigative services. Many a thief and molester has found himself suddenly in the clutches of the law and on the way to the penitentiary when he discovered that the woman he approached was a police officer with full power and authority—and ability!

The services of a policewoman are particularly useful in the general area of delinquency and crime prevention. Here, they perform investigative and social-service oriented activities for women, teenage females and pre-teen youngsters, both male and female.

A policewoman with the proper qualifications can on occasion virtually perform miracles with the youngster beset with problems—

social, mental or physical, or a combination of all three. Bringing the clinical resources of the community into contact with a developing behavior problem case in its early stages, a life pattern may be reshaped and redirected into more constructive channels.

Use of Civilians in the Smaller Department

As of 1965, 10.7 percent of the total personnel in police departments were civilians.[1] This represents an increase of nearly 3 percent over the total used in 1960. For example, most of the larger departments are now using "meter maids" to enforce parking regulations.

There are a number of routine tasks in a police department that can be performed by civilians, including various types of clerical duties and work assignments in the records unit. It is sound practice, particularly in the smaller departments, to give such assignments to civilians and release uniformed officers for patrol. Civilian personnel should be selected with care and where practicable, on the basis of a competitive examination. Since their assignment may give them access to police records, a thorough background investigation is a prerequisite to employment.

Conditions of Service

Promotion. Promotion is one of the most important mechanisms in the entire field of personnel management. It serves two major purposes: first, through the avenue of promotion, supervisory, command personnel and administrative officers are selected; secondly, it gives expression to the opportunity for personal achievement, with all that can mean in terms of morale and initiative.

In the American police field, it is now standard practice in virtually every department to award promotion on the basis of merit, as determined by competitive examination. Seniority must be relegated to a background position as a minor factor. The examination should include, in addition to written tests, the following:

1. The officer's prior performance record.

---

[1] U. S. Department of Justice, Federal Bureau of Investigation, *Uniform Crime Reports,* U. S. Printing Office, Washington, D. C., 1966, p. 132.

2. The results of rating by superior officers.
3. The officer's educational background.
4. Demonstrated qualities of leadership potential and the ability to assume greater responsibility.

The contents of an officer's personnel folder become an indispensable tool as he comes under consideration for promotion.

Here again, it must be reemphasized that the development of lateral mobility or lateral entry of police personnel is geared directly to the dimensions of the promotional process.

The fringe benefits in police service today are competitive with business and industry. The forty-hour work week is now standard throughout the country. Some departments provide compensation for overtime, but this is the exception rather than the rule. Under the inspired leadership of Chief August Vollmer in the Police Department of Berkeley, California, his officers seldom observed strictly the eight-hour tour of duty; it was frequently twelve to fifteen and the compensation was the satisfaction of loyal service to the chief and department.

It is the practice in virtually every police department to accumulate sick leave at the rate of one day for each month of service up to a maximum of six months, exclusive of Saturdays and Sundays, or other regular days off. It must be observed that the effective personnel strength of too many departments is depleted by time lost due to illness. As previously indicated, this can be drastically reduced by the use of extreme care in the recruiting process. An annual vacation of at least two weeks, exclusive of regular days off, is now standard practice in the American police field.

Coupled with the foregoing conditions of service, provision for the retirement of police personnel is a regular feature of police departments throughout the country. Pension plans, of course, vary from one department to the other. One thing is certain—a department should determine through those competent to judge that its pension program is actuarilly sound.

In order to foster the development of lateral mobility of police personnel, a nationwide police retirement system must be established which will permit the transfer of retirement credit from one department to another.[2] There is ample precedent for a national police retirement program. For example, the Teachers Insurance and Annuity Association of America blankets the nation's academic system with a retirement and pension program second to none. A university or college faculty member may transfer his retirement credit at will from one educational institution to another. These matters will no doubt be receiving the attenion of police departments and police associations in the forseeable future.

APPENDIX A
Announcement of Competitive Examination
for Position of
Chief of Police, Seattle, Washington

The City of Seattle announces a nationwide, open competitive examination for the position listed above, which will be filled through appointment by the Mayor from a list of three eligible candidates recommended by the examining board. Selection will be based upon the results of the competitive examination.

Final Date for Filing Applications

Applications must be filed in the office of Mr. Kenneth Colman, Chairman of the Police Advisory Committee, Colman Building, Seattle, Washington, on or before 5:00 p.m., or post-marked not later than midnight, May 15, 1946. To secure application form, wire Mayor's Office, Seattle 4, Washington.

Examination Date

Written examination—Friday, May 31, 1946.
Oral examination—June 24 to 29 inclusive.

Place of Examination

For the convenience of applicants in the several geographic areas of the nation, written examinations will be held at the following locations:

Institute of Government	Department of Political Science
University of Washington	University of California
Seattle, Washington	Berkeley, California
Traffic Institute	Department of Legal Medicine
Northwestern University	Harvard University
Evanston, Illinois	Cambridge, Massachusetts

Bureau of Municipal Research
University of Texas
Austin, Texas

And other such places throughout the United States as the number of applicants and conditions require. The oral examination will be held in Seattle, Washington only.

Only those candidates whose experience and written examinations satisfy the examining board will be called to Seattle for the oral examination. The oral interview will be supplemented by a confidential investigation of the character and professional record of candidates who qualify. Competitors who attain an eligible rating may be investigated with the object of securing additional evidence as to their qualifications and fitness for this position, and to secure evidence as to their honesty, integrity, habits, loyalty and general character.

Applicants called to Seattle for oral examination will defray their own expenses.

The decisions of the examining board in the selection of three eligible candidates will be final.

Salary
Minimum, $7,500.00 per year.

Tenure Of Office
Indefinite tenure.

Qualifications
Not less than ten years full time employment in public safety or law enforcement work within the last 15 years, of which a part must have been in an administrative capacity. The nature and extent of the applicant's administrative experience are considered of the highest importance. In considering the length of time served

in public safety and law enforcement organizations, time spent on leave of absence in the Armed Forces will be considered as continuous service.

Military experience, especially at command levels, is conceded to be an asset to a police executive and careful consideration will therefore be given to the applicant's military service record.

Education

Equivalent to that represented by completion of the twelfth grade or graduation from high school. College level training in public administration, police science and administration, criminal law, psychology, sociology, economics or business administration, or a combination of these fields of study, may be substituted for not more than two years of the required experience. In evaluating experience, major consideration will be given to the quality, importance and breadth of experience rather than to years of experience.

Age Limit

Applicants for this position must have reached their 32nd birthday on the closing date for receipt of applications specified at the head of this announcement.

Duties of Position

The duties of this position include the following:

1. Organization of the Seattle Police Department over a period of five years in accordance with professional standards.
2. Planning and execution of a professional police program for the protection of life and property, preservation of peace and order, conrol and prevention of crime and vice, and the regulation and control of traffic.
3. Planning and direction of the total organization and operations of a metropolitan Police Department.
4. Selection and appointment, subject to Civil Service provisions, of officers and employees best qualified to carry on the police program, and supervision of their training, assignment and performance.

5. Interpretation of police policies and objectives to personnel of the Department, the public and the press.
6. Such other duties as may be necessary in the projection of police service in Seattle, on a professional career basis.

Applications are invited from qualified applicants throughout the United States.

Examining Board

CHARLES W. DUL-
LEA
Western Vice President,
International Ass'n
Chiefs of Police
Chief of Police
San Francisco, Calif.

COL. HOMER GAR-
RISON, Jr.
Director,
State Department of
Public Safety
Fourth Vice President,
International Ass'n
Chiefs of Police
Austin, Texas.

V. A. LEONARD,
Chairman
Department of Police
Science and Adminis⁻
tration
State College of Wash-
ington
Pullman, Washington

ADDRESS ALL APPLICATIONS TO:
KENNETH B. COLMAN, Chairman
Police Advisory Committee
Colman Building
Seattle 4, Washington

CITY OF SEATTLE, WASHINGTON
Application for the Position of Police Chief

Application No. . . . .
Date received . . . . ·· . . . .

General Instructions

Applications must be typewritten or in ink, sworn to before a notary or other officer authorized to administer oaths and filed in the office of Kenneth B. Colman, Chairman of the Police Advisory Comittee, Colman Building, Seattle, on or before 5:00 p.m., or postmarked not later than midnight, May 15, 1946.

Applicants should read carefully the announcement in the bulletin submitted with this form.

It is important that each statement or answer in this application be complete, truthful and accurate. Incomplete, false or misleading statements or answers may be cause for rejection. Where spaces on this blank are insufficient, supply additional information on bond paper 8½ x 11 size.

1. Name .... Address ....
2. Age ...... Place and date of birth ....
   U.S. Citizen? ....
3. Marital status .... Number of children ......
4. Height .... Weight (in street clothes) ....
5. Is your health such as to enable you to perform regularly the duties of this position?
6. Have you any defect of hearing, sight, speech or limb? (Eligible candidates will be given a medical examination in Seattle at time of oral interview)
7. Are you addicted to the moderate or immoderate use of alcohol, or to the use of drugs in any form?
8. Have you ever been arrested, indicted or convicted for any law violation other than a minor traffic offense?
9. Have you ever been discharged or forced to resign from a position?
10. Education. (Give details)
    Grammar and High School
    College or University
    Post-graduate work
11. Courses completed in the fields of public administration and police administration. (Give details of university or college program)
12. Special honors received
13. Military experience and record
14. Publications authored (books, articles, reports—give exact titles and references)
15. Professional associations to which you belong
16. List any income other than your present salary
17. List all business interests or connections outside of police service
18. List all organizations to which you belong as a member
19. Positions of professional or civic leadership which you have

held

20. Employment record. Present and former employments. (Beginning with present or latest employment, list in reverse order all positions held for the last fifteen years, stating in each case reason for leaving previous position. Use separate sheet of paper)

21. For each of the above positions in police work give a brief description of the principal tasks you performed, the number of employees supervised by you, the assistance and supervision required from your superiors, and any other information indicating the nature and responsibilities of the position.

22. Write a brief personal statement commenting upon significant aspects of your professional experience and educational training which in your judgment qualify you to discharge with distinction the duties and responsibilities of this position

23. Do you object to the Committee making inquiry of your present employer regarding your character and qualifications?

24. Names, addresses and occupations of five persons, not relatives, nor employers, nor supervisors, who have knowledge of your character and ability

25. Attach to this application a 5 x 7 photograph of yourself and one set of fingerprints. These are a part of your application.

. . . .
Signature of Applicant

Affidavit

State of . . . .

County of . . . .

On this . . . . . . day of . . . ., 1946, before me personally appeared . . . . who stated on oath that he is the author of this application and that the information contained therein is true and correct to the best of his knowledge and belief.

Witness my hand and seal.

. . . .
Notary Public.

APPENDIX B

The City of Berkeley
Berkeley, California

ANNOUNCES CONTINUOUS OPEN COMPETITIVE
EXAMINATIONS FOR PATROLMEN
$628 - $693

Qualified and ambitious young men are invited to apply for career positions in an outstanding police department.

Patrolmen may be assigned to either the Patrol, Detective, or Service divisions. Patrolmen assigned to the Patrol Division are responsible for crime prevention and for investigation, from complaint to solution, of all cases within their patrol areas. Patrol areas are rotated to provide the officer with a wide variety of police experience. When assigned to the Detective Division, Patrolmen assist in criminal investigations which involve several patrol areas. Patrolmen assigned to the Service Division work in records, identification, dispatching, jail supervision, and operate an emergency ambulance.

Patrolmen receive excellent training in all phases of police work. Working conditions are excellent and include paid vacations, sick leave, membership in a retirement system, and promotion from the ranks through examinations.

How to Qualify: File an application with the Personnel Department if you meet the following requirements:

    Are between the ages of 20 and 29 by the final date of filing application

    Have successfully completed the equivalent of 2 years (60 semester hours or 90 quarter hours) in an accredited college or university

    Have a valid Motor Vehicle Operator's License and a good driving record

    Are at least 5'9" in height, without shoes, and have proportionate weight

    Are in good general health and physical condition, including uncorrected vision of at least 20/40 in both eyes correctable to 20/20; good color vision

Have a personal history above reproach

Candidates must earn a score of 70% or better on each part of the examination, which consists of:

Written test 60%

Interview 40%

Mental aptitude test ....Qualifying

Physical agility test ....Qualifying

The qualifying physical agility test consists of four events. Candidates must be successful in *each* of the following events: 7-foot standing broad jump; 7 pull-ups; 30 sit-ups; and an obstacle course which must be completed within 48 seconds.

Successful Candidates who earn a final grade of 70% or better will have their names entered on an open-continuous employment list from which appointments are made. Persons selected for appointment must pass a medical examination by a City physician prior to appointment. A loyalty oath is administered, and a background investigation completed before appointment. No candidate will be appointed until he has reached his 21st birthday, and no candidate will be appointed who has reached his 30th birthday. APPLICATIONS MAY BE OBTAINED BY WRITING THE PERSONNEL DEPARTMENT, 2100 GROVE STREET, BERKELEY, OR BY CALLING THORNWALL 1-6076 IN BERKELEY

BERKELEY RESIDENCE IS NOT REQUIRED TO QUALIFY FOR THIS POSITION

UNITED STATES CITIZENSHIP IS REQUIRED TO QUALIFY FOR THIS POSITION

7/1/63

ANSWER ALL QUESTIONS USE INK OR TYPEWRITER	CITY OF BERKELEY APPLICATION FOR EMPLOYMENT	DATE FILED
		MONTH DAY YEAR

INSTRUCTIONS

FILL OUT THIS APPLICATION COMPLETELY AND ACCURATELY. IF YOUR APPLICATION IS MADE OUT PROPERLY IT MAY INCREASE YOUR CHANCES FOR EMPLOYMENT. ALL STATEMENTS IN YOUR APPLICATION ARE SUBJECT TO VERIFICATION. INCORRECT STATEMENT MAY BAR OR REMOVE YOU FROM EMPLOYMENT.
(Be sure the application is signed at the bottom of this page.)

1. YOUR NAME? (PRINT)

FIRST   MIDDLE   LAST

2. FOR WHAT POSITION ARE YOU APPLYING?
(GIVE EXACT TITLE.)

3. YOUR ADDRESS? (PRINT)

NUMBER   STREET   CITY   STATE

YOUR PHONE NUMBER?
HOME
BUSINESS

4. ARE YOU A U.S. CITIZEN?
(ONLY U.S. CITIZENS ARE ELIGIBLE TO APPLY)
YES ☐   NO ☐

5. WHO SHOULD BE NOTIFIED IN CASE OF EMERGENCY?
NAME
ADDRESS   TELEPHONE

6. WHEN WERE YOU BORN?
MONTH   DAY   YEAR

7. SEX
MALE ☐
FEMALE ☐

8. ARE YOU
SINGLE ___
MARRIED ___
WIDOWED ___
DIVORCED ___

9.
YOUR WEIGHT? ___ LBS.
YOUR HEIGHT? ___ FT. IN.

10. WERE YOU EVER DISCHARGED OR FORCED TO RESIGN BECAUSE OF MISCONDUCT OR UNSATISFACTORY SERVICES?
YES ☐
NO ☐
IF SO, STATE CIRCUMSTANCES INCLUDING NAMES AND ADDRESSES OF EMPLOYERS ON THE BACK OF THIS APPLICATION.

11. MAY WE CONTACT YOUR PRESENT EMPLOYER AS TO YOUR QUALIFICATIONS, CHARACTER, ETC.?
(We shall contact him only if you permit it.)
PLEASE DON'T ☐
DON'T MIND ☐
PLEASE DO ☐

12. WILL YOU ACCEPT TEMPORARY WORK?
YES ☐   NO ☐

13. HAVE YOU EVER BEEN ARRESTED, INDICTED, CONVICTED, IMPRISONED, PLACED ON PROBATION OR REQUIRED TO PAY A FINE OF MORE THAN $25.00?
YES ☐   NO ☐
IF SO, GIVE DATE, PLACE AND NATURE OF EACH OFFENSE ON REVERSE SIDE. IF IN DOUBT, STATE DETAILS. YOUR ANSWER TO THIS QUESTION MAY BE CHECKED WITH THE FBI. AN UNTRUE ANSWER WILL DISQUALIFY YOU.

14. HAVE YOU EVER RECEIVED WORKMEN'S COMPENSATION?
YES ☐   NO ☐
IF SO, GIVE DATE AND NATURE OF EACH INJURY OR ILLNESS.

15. IF YOU ARE REQUIRED TO POSSESS A LICENSE OR CERTIFICATE IN ORDER TO QUALIFY FOR THE POSITION FOR WHICH YOU ARE APPLYING, WHAT IS THE NAME AND NUMBER OF SUCH, AND WHAT IS THE NAME OF THE LICENSING BOARD? (INCLUDE DRIVER'S LICENSE)
NAME OF LICENSE OR CERTIFICATE NUMBER
NAME OF LICENSING BOARD

16. IF YOU HAVE BEEN DISCHARGED OR SEPARATED FROM THE ARMED FORCES WITHIN THE PAST FIVE (5) YEARS, YOU MAY BE ENTITLED TO VETERANS' PREFERENCE. TO BE CONSIDERED FOR SUCH PREFERENCE, YOU MUST SUBMIT A CERTIFIED COPY OF YOUR DISCHARGE PAPERS PRIOR TO THE CLOSING DATE FOR FILING APPLICATIONS. IF YOU ARE A DISABLED VETERAN, YOU SHOULD SUBMIT A CERTIFICATE WHICH SHOWS AT LEAST TEN PERCENT DISABILITY TO EXIST AT THE TIME OF APPLICATION.

17.   **CERTIFICATE OF APPLICANT**

I HEREBY CERTIFY THAT ALL STATEMENTS MADE IN THIS APPLICATION ARE TRUE, AND COMPLETE, AND THAT ANY MISSTATEMENTS OF MATERIAL FACTS WILL SUBJECT ME TO DISQUALIFICATION OR DISMISSAL.

SIGNATURE OF CANDIDATE

SUBMIT TO: PERSONNEL DEPARTMENT, ROOM 19, CITY HALL, BERKELEY, CALIFORNIA.

18. EDUCATION

CIRCLE HIGHEST GRADE COMPLETED	NAME OF SCHOOL		LOCATION	GRADUATE?	DATE
1 2 3 4 5 6 7 8 9 10 11 12					

COLLEGES OR UNIVERSITIES ATTENDED	ATTENDANCE DATES	TOTAL SEMESTER UNITS	DEGREE AND YEAR	MAJOR SUBJECT	SEMESTER UNITS IN MAJOR SUBJECTS
OTHER (NAME)					

RELATED INFORMATION

19. EXPERIENCE

LIST ALL JOBS YOU HAVE HELD IN THE LAST TEN YEARS. PUT YOUR PRESENT OR MOST RECENT JOB FIRST. BY BEING COMPLETE YOU MAY IMPROVE YOUR CHANCES FOR EMPLOYMENT. IF YOU NEED MORE SPACE, YOU MAY ATTACH ADDITIONAL SHEETS.   INCLUDE MILITARY SERVICE.

FROM MONTH YEAR TO MONTH YEAR	EXACT TITLE OF POSITION:	
NAME AND ADDRESS OF EMPLOYER	YOUR DUTIES ARE:	
NAME AND TITLE OF YOUR SUPERVISOR		
REASON FOR LEAVING	NUMBER SUPERVISED	SALARY PER MO.

FROM TO	EXACT TITLE OF POSITION:	
NAME AND ADDRESS OF EMPLOYER	YOUR DUTIES WERE:	
NAME AND TITLE OF YOUR SUPERVISOR		
REASON FOR LEAVING	NUMBER SUPERVISED	SALARY PER MO.

FROM TO	EXACT TITLE OF POSITION:	
NAME AND ADDRESS OF EMPLOYER	YOUR DUTIES WERE:	
NAME AND TITLE OF YOUR SUPERVISOR		
REASON FOR LEAVING	NUMBER SUPERVISED	SALARY PER MO.

FROM TO	EXACT TITLE OF POSITION:	
NAME AND ADDRESS OF EMPLOYER	YOUR DUTIES WERE:	
NAME AND TITLE OF YOUR SUPERVISOR		
REASON FOR LEAVING	NUMBER SUPERVISED	SALARY PER MO.

FROM TO	EXACT TITLE OF POSITION:	
NAME AND ADDRESS OF EMPLOYER	YOUR DUTIES WERE:	
NAME AND TITLE OF YOUR SUPERVISOR		
REASON FOR LEAVING	NUMBER SUPERVISED	SALARY PER MO.

REMARKS:

306-678

The City of Berkeley
Berkeley, California
POLICE TRAINEE

$2.00 – $2.10 – $2.20 per hour

Police Trainees assist regular Berkeley Police Officers in performing a variety of duties. Among the duties that a Police Trainee may perform are: accepting and processing complaints received at the public counter or by telephone; performing routine jail duties; operating teletype and radio dispatching equipment; performing some of the routine technical tasks in the identification bureau, crime and photography laboratory; writing reports; and aiding in the transporting, searching, booking and processing of prisoners. Each Police Trainee receives 40 hours of intensive training before he is assigned to the Service Division.

Police Trainees work three 8-hour shifts one week and two 8-hour shifts the following week, for an average work week of 20 hours.

The standards for Police Trainee, with the exception of age, are the same as those for Patrolman. Upon reaching 21 years of age, a Police Trainee may be appointed as a Patrolman without further examination. Candidates selected for appointment are encouraged to accept full-time appointments with the Police Department for a minimum period of three years, excluding absence for military service, following completion of their academic program.

HOW TO QUALIFY: File an application with the Personnel Department if you meet the following requirements:

> Are between the ages of 18 and 26 by the final date of filing application
> Are presently enrolled in good standing as a junior or senior student in an accredited four-year college or university
> Have a valid California Motor Vehicle Operator's License and a good driving record
> Are at least 5'9" in height, without shoes, and have proportionate weight
> Are in good general health and physical condition, including uncorrected vision of at least 20/40 in both eyes correctable to 20/20; good color vision
> Have a personal history above reproach
> Be able to type at least 30 net words per minute.

Candidates must earn a score of 70% or better on each part of the examination, which consists of the following:

Written test	_____60%	Physical agility test	_Qualifying
Interview	_____40%	Typing test	_____Qualifying

The qualifying physical agility test consists of four events. Candidates must be successful in each of the following events: 7-foot standing broad jump, 7 pull-ups, 30 sit-ups, and an obstacle course which must be completed within 48 seconds.

SUCCESSFUL CANDIDATES   will have their names entered on an employment list from which appointments are made. Persons selected for appointment must pass a medical examination by a City physician prior to appointment. A loyalty oath is administered, and a comprehensive background investigation completed before appointment.

APPLICATIONS MAY BE OBTAINED BY WRITING THE PERSONNEL DEPARTMENT, 2100 GROVE STREET, BERKELEY, OR BY CALLING THORNWALL 1-6076 IN BERKELEY.

BERKELEY RESIDENCE IS NOT REQUIRED TO QUALIFY FOR THIS POSITION
UNITED STATES CITIZENSHIP IS REQUIRED TO QUALIFY FOR THIS POSITION

7/3/63

DATE FILED

POLICE DEPARTMENT
CITY OF BERKELEY

Month   Day   Year

PERSONAL HISTORY QUESTIONNAIRE

INSTRUCTIONS

Fill out this questionnaire completely and accurately. If your questionnaire is made out properly it may increase your chances for employment. All statements in your questionnaire are subject to verification. Incorrect statements may bar or remove you from employment. If space provided is inadequate, add another page and identify additional information by item number.

1. YOUR NAME? (Print)

      FIRST   MIDDLE   LAST

2. Give any other names you have used or been known by, and attach a statement giving reasons (if none, so state)

YOUR PHONE NUMBER
HOME _____
BUSINESS _____

3. YOUR ADDRESS? (Print)

  NUMBER   STREET   CITY   STATE

4. WITH WHOM DO YOU RESIDE? _____

5. WHEN WERE YOU BORN? _____   6. WHERE WERE YOU BORN?

     MONTH   DAY   YEAR

     CITY   STATE   COUNTY

7. ARE YOU SINGLE, MARRIED, SEPARATED OR DIVORCED? _____

8. IF SINGLE, DO YOU LIVE WITH YOUR PARENTS? _____ YES OR NO _____

9. GIVE FOLLOWING INFORMATION REGARDING MARRIAGE, OR MARRIAGES:

WHEN	WHERE	BY WHOM	WIFE'S MAIDEN NAME

10. GIVE FOLLOWING INFORMATION CONCERNING YOUR PARENTS AND YOUR SPOUSES' PARENTS:

NAME	ADDRESS	LIVING?	WHERE BORN
FATHER			
MOTHER'S MAIDEN			
FATHER-IN-LAW			
MOTHER-IN-LAW			

11. ARE YOU LIVING WITH YOUR WIFE? _____ YES OR NO _____

12. IF NOT, STATE REASONS _____

13. WERE YOU EVER LEGALLY OR VOLUNTARILY SEPARATED? _____YES or NO _____
    HOW MANY TIMES? _____

14. WERE YOU EVER DIVORCED OR HAD A MARRIAGE ANNULLED?_____ YES or NO _____
    HOW MANY TIMES? _____

15. IF A MARRIAGE TO WHICH YOU WERE A PARTY WAS EVER DISSOLVED, FILL OUT THE FOLLOWING:

HOW	TO WHOM WAS DIVORCE GRANTED
SEPARATED	
DIVORCED	
ANNULLED	

16. LIST BELOW EVERY CHILD BORN TO YOU:

NAME	DATE OF BIRTH	PLACE OF BIRTH	WITH WHOM AND WHERE RESIDES?

17. ARE YOU NOW SUPPORTING ALL CHILDREN BORN TO YOU, ADOPTED BY YOU AND STEPCHILDREN?
    _____ YES OR NO _____
    IF NOT, GIVE FULL DETAILS _____
    _____
    _____
    _____

18. HAVE YOU EVER BEEN INVOLVED AS DEFENDANT IN A PATERNITY PROCEEDING ____YES, NO____
    IF YES, STATE FULL DETAILS _____
    _____
    _____
    _____

19. HAS ANY MEMBER OF YOUR IMMEDIATE FAMILY EVER BEEN ARRESTED FOR OR CONVICTED OF A
    FELONY CRIME? _____YES NO:____   IF YES, GIVE PARTICULARS BELOW

NAME	RELATIONSHIP	CRIME COMMITTED	WHERE ARRESTED

20. GIVE THE NAMES OF EVERY MEMBER OF YOUR IMMEDIATE FAMILY WHO IS STILL LIVING: INCLUDE FATHER, MOTHER, SISTERS, BROTHERS, UNCLES, AUNTS.

NAME	RELATIONSHIP	ADDRESS	OCCUPATION

21. HAS ANY MEMBER OF YOUR IMMEDIATE FAMILY EVER BEEN TREATED FOR A NERVOUS OR MENTAL DISORDER? _____ YES OR NO _____: IF YES, GIVE PARTICULARS BELOW

NAME	RELATIONSHIP	NATURE OF ILLNESS	WHERE & BY WHOM TRT'D

22. ARE YOU A CITIZEN OF THE UNITED STATES? _____YES NO_____: (Only U.S. Citizens are eligible to apply: If not a native born citizen, present naturalization papers.)
NATURAL BORN: ____ NATURALIZED _____ DERIVATIVE _____

23. HAVE YOU EVER BY WORD OF MOUTH OR IN WRITING ADVOCATED, ADVISED, OR TAUGHT THE DOCTRINE THAT THE GOVERNMENT OF THE UNITED STATES OF AMERICA OR OF ANY STATE OR ANY POLITICAL SUBDIVISION THEREOF SHOULD BE OVERTHROWN OR OVERTURNED BY FORCE, VIOLENCE, OR ANY UNLAWFUL MEANS? _____ YES OR NO_____

24. ARE YOU NOW OR HAVE YOU EVER BEEN A MEMBER OF ANY SUBVERSIVE ORGANIZATION ?
_____YES NO _____

25. HAVE YOU EVER BEEN CONNECTED OR AFFILIATED IN ANY MANNER WITH OR HAVE YOU EVER ATTENDED ANY MEETINGS OF ANY SUBVERSIVE ORGANIZATION? _____YES NO_____ IF YES, DESCRIBE THE CIRCUMSTANCES AND REASONS FOR ATTENDANCE.

_____

_____

_____

RESIDENCES

26. LIST ADDRESSES SINCE YOUR TENTH BIRTHDAY, STARTING WITH PRESENT ADDRESS AT TOP

FROM MO. YR.		TO MO. YR.		ADDRESS OF RESIDENCE	CITY AND STATE	FROM WHOM RENTED INCLUDE ADDRESS

EMPLOYMENT

27. WHAT IS YOUR OCCUPATION OR CALLING ? _____

28. ARE YOU NOW OR HAVE YOU EVER BEEN ENGAGED IN ANY BUSINESS AS AN OWNER, PARTNER, OR CORPORATE MEMBER ? _____YES OR NO _____: IF YES, GIVE DETAILS BELOW:

_____

_____

_____

29. WHAT IS YOUR SOCIAL SECURITY NUMBER ? _____

30. WERE YOU EVER DISCHARGED OR FORCED TO RESIGN BECAUSE OF MISCONDUCT OR UNSATISFACTORY SERVICE ? _____YES OR NO _____: IF YES, GIVE DETAILS BELOW:

_____

31. HAVE YOUR EMPLOYERS ALWAYS TREATED YOU FAIRLY ? _____YES OR NO_____: IF NOT, EXPLAIN

_____

32. DO YOU OBJECT TO WEARING A UNIFORM ? _____YES OR NO _____

33. DO YOU OBJECT TO WORKING NIGHTS ? _____ YES OR NO _____

34. HAVE YOU HAD EXPERIENCE WITH SHIFT WORK ? _____YES OR NO _____

35. HAVE YOU EVER FILED A CLAIM FOR WORKMAN'S COMPENSATION ? _____ YES   NO_____: IF YES, GIVE DETAILS BELOW:

_____

_____

_____

_____

_____

36. List all jobs you have held in the last ten years. Put your present or most recent job first. By being complete you may improve your chances for employment. If you need more space, you may attach additional sheets. Include military service in proper time sequence and temporary part-time jobs.

FROM_____TO _____   EXACT TITLE OF POSITION_____
    Month and Year   Month and Year

NAME AND ADDRESS OF EMPLOYER   YOUR DUTIES ARE:

NAME & TITLE OF YOUR SUPERVISOR

REASON FOR LEAVING   NUMBER SUPERVISED   SALARY PER
    MONTH:

FROM_____TO _____   EXACT TITLE OF POSITION_____
    Month and Year   Month and Year

NAME AND ADDRESS OF EMPLOYER   YOUR DUTIES WERE:

NAME & TITLE OF YOUR SUPERVISOR

REASON FOR LEAVING   NUMBER SUPERVISED   SALARY PER
    MONTH:

FROM_____TO _____   EXACT TITLE OF POSITION_____
    Month and Year   Month and Year

NAME AND ADDRESS OF EMPLOYER   YOUR DUTIES WERE:

36. **CONTINUED ....**

List all jobs you have held in the last ten years. Put your present or most recent job first. By being complete you may improve your chances for employment. If you need more space, you may attach additional sheets. Include military service in proper time sequence and temporary part-time jobs.

FROM_____TO _____   EXACT TITLE OF POSITION_____
    Month and Year   Month and Year

NAME AND ADDRESS OF EMPLOYER   YOUR DUTIES ARE:

NAME & TITLE OF YOUR SUPERVISOR

REASON FOR LEAVING   NUMBER SUPERVISED   SALARY PER
    MONTH:

FROM_____TO _____   EXACT TITLE OF POSITION_____
    Month and Year   Month and Year

NAME AND ADDRESS OF EMPLOYER   YOUR DUTIES WERE:

NAME & TITLE OF YOUR SUPERVISOR

REASON FOR LEAVING   NUMBER SUPERVISED   SALARY PER
    MONTH:

FROM_____TO _____   EXACT TITLE OF POSITION_____
    Month and Year   Month and Year

NAME & TITLE OF YOUR SUPERVISOR

REASON FOR LEAVING   NUMBER SUPERVISED   SALARY PER
                                                                          MONTH:

FROM_____TO_____   EXACT TITLE OF POSITION_____
      Month and Year   Month and Year

NAME AND ADDRESS OF EMPLOYER   YOUR DUTIES WERE:

NAME & TITLE OF YOUR SUPERVISOR

REASON FOR LEAVING   NUMBER SUPERVISED   SALARY PER
                                                                          MONTH:

FROM_____TO_____   EXACT TITLE OF POSITION_____
      Month and Year   Month and Year

NAME AND ADDRESS OF EMPLOYER   YOUR DUTIES WERE:

NAME & TITLE OF YOUR SUPERVISOR

REASON FOR LEAVING   NUMBER SUPERVISED   SALARY PER
                                                                          MONTH:

37. DO YOU HAVE ANY PHYSICAL DISABILITIES AT THIS TIME OR HAVE YOU EVER HAD ANY ?
          _____YES OR NO_____: IF YES, GIVE DETAILS BELOW:
          _____
          _____
          _____

38. LIST BELOW ANY EXTENDED ABSENCES FROM WORK YOU HAVE HAD BECAUSE OF PERSONAL ILLNESS
          AND DESCRIBE THE CAUSES: _____
          _____
          _____
          _____
          _____

39. LIST BELOW EVERY CIVIL SERVICE COMPETITIVE EXAMINATION YOU HAVE TAKEN. IF NONE,
          SO STATE.

AGENCY	APPROXIMATE DATE OF EXAM.	POSITION ON LIST	STATUS

NAME AND ADDRESS OF EMPLOYER	YOUR DUTIES WERE:	
NAME & TITLE OF YOUR SUPERVISOR		
REASON FOR LEAVING	NUMBER SUPERVISED	SALARY PER MONTH:

FROM_____ TO _____ EXACT TITLE OF POSITION_____
　　　Month and Year　　　Month and Year

NAME AND ADDRESS OF EMPLOYER	YOUR DUTIES WERE:	
NAME & TITLE OF YOUR SUPERVISOR		
REASON FOR LEAVING	NUMBER SUPERVISED	SALARY PER MONTH:

FROM_____TO _____ EXACT TITLE OF POSITION_____
　　　Month and Year　　　Month and Year

NAME AND ADDRESS OF EMPLOYER	YOUR DUTIES WERE:	
NAME & TITLE OF YOUR SUPERVISOR		
REASON FOR LEAVING	NUMBER SUPERVISED	SALARY PER MONTH:

40. ARE YOU NOW ON ANY ELIGIBILITY LIST ? _____ YES   NO _____: IF YES, LIST BELOW:
_____
_____
_____

41. IF YOU WERE EVER PLACED ON AN ELIGIBILITY LIST AND WERE NOT HIRED, STATE WHY:
_____
_____
_____
_____

42. WERE YOU EVER REJECTED FOR ANY CIVIL SERVICE POSITION ? _____YES NO_____: IF YES,
WHY ? _____
_____
_____
_____

43. HAVE YOU EVER PREVIOUSLY SUBMITTED AN APPLICATION FOR APPOINTMENT TO THE BERKELEY
POLICE DEPARTMENT ? _____YES NO_____: APPROXIMATE DATE: _____

44. HAVE YOU EVER RECEIVED UNEMPLOYMENT INSURANCE OR OTHER FEDERAL, STATE OR LOCAL BENEFITS OR ASSISTANCE? _____YES   NO_____.

KIND	LOCAL OFFICE	ADDRESS	FOR HOW LONG?

45. IN THE SPACE PROVIDED BELOW LIST YOUR REASONS FOR APPLYING FOR THIS POSITION:

_____

_____

_____

_____

MILITARY STATUS

If you have served with the Armed Forces during the past five (5) years, Veterans Preference may be given if honorably discharged.

46. HAVE YOU EVER SERVED IN A MILITARY OR NAVAL ORGANIZATION OF THE UNITED STATES? _____YES   NO_____

47. GIVE BRANCH OF SERVICE _____ COMPANY_____
REGIMENT_____ DIVISION_____ SHIP _____

48. WHAT IS YOUR SERVICE NUMBER?_____

49. HIGHEST RANK HELD _____

50. HOW MANY PERIODS OF ACTIVE MILITARY SERVICE HAVE YOU HAD?_____

51. LIST ALL MEDALS AND DECORATIONS AWARDED YOU AS A MEMBER OF THE ARMED FORCES:

_____

_____

_____

52. WHAT IS THE TYPE OF YOUR DISCHARGE? HONORABLE, DISHONORABLE, MEDICAL, HONORABLE CONDITIONS, ETC.? BE EXACT _____

53. GIVE DATE AND LOCATION OF ENTRANCE TO ACTIVE DUTY _____

54. GIVE DATE AND LOCATION OF DISCHARGE _____

55. IF YOU HAVE HAD NO MILITARY SERVICE, GIVE REASONS _____

_____

56. WERE YOU EVER COURT-MARTIALED, TRIED ON CHARGES, OR WERE YOU THE SUBJECT OF A SUMMARY COURT, DECK COURT, CAPTAIN'S MAST OR COMPANY PUNISHMENT, OR ANY OTHER DISCIPLINARY ACTION WHILE A MEMBER OF THE ARMED FORCES?_____YES   NO_____: IF YES, EXPLAIN BELOW:_____

_____

_____

57. GIVE PERIOD OR PERIODS OF ACTIVE MILITARY SERVICE:

From _____ To _____ From _____ To _____

From _____ To _____ From _____ To _____

From _____ To _____ From _____ To _____

58. ARE YOU NOW OR WERE YOU EVER AN ACTIVE OR INACTIVE MEMBER OF ANY BRANCH OF THE UNITED STATES RESERVE FORCES? _____YES NO _____ STATE WHICH: ACTIVE OR INACTIVE _____

59. BRANCH _____ UNIT _____ RANK_____

ADDRESS _____ FROM _____ TO _____

60. ARE YOU NOW, OR WERE YOU EVER, A MEMBER OF THE NATIONAL GUARD? _____YES NO_____

61. STATE _____ REGIMENT_____ UNIT_____RANK_____

FROM_____ TO _____ TYPE OF DISCHARGE_____

62. LIST ANY DISCIPLINARY ACTION TAKEN AGAINST YOU IN THE NATIONAL GUARD OR OTHER RESERVE UNIT. _____

_____

_____

EDUCATION

63. INDICATE ON FORM BELOW, THE VARIOUS SCHOOLS YOU HAVE ATTENDED AND OTHER INFOR - MATION REQUESTED. IF YOU CANNOT REMEMBER, SAY SO. DO NOT TROUBLE TO WRITE THE SCHOOL FOR INFORMATION.

NAME ADDRESS (CITY AND STATE)	NO. FULL YRS. WORK COMPLETED	WHEN ATTENDED	GRADUATE	PRINCIPAL OR DEAN
GRAMMAR SCHOOLS_____				
JUNIOR HIGH _____ SCHOOLS				
HIGH _____ SCHOOLS				
UNIVERSITY _____ OR _____ COLLEGES_____				

53. SCHOOLS **(Continued)**

NAME ADDRESS (CITY AND STATE)	NO. FULL YEARS WORK COMPLETED	WHEN ATTENDED	GRADUATED	PRINCIPAL OR DEAN
BUSINESS COLLEGES				
EXTENSION OR CORRESPONDENCE COURSES				

HIGH SCHOOL	SUBJECTS TAKEN	GRADES

JUNIOR COLLEGE COLLEGE OR UNIVERSITY	SUBJECTS TAKEN	GRADES

64. WHAT SCHOOL SUBJECTS WERE MOST DIFFICULT FOR YOU?

65. WHAT SCHOOL SUBJECTS DID YOU LIKE BEST?

66. WERE YOU EVER EXPELLED OR SUSPENDED FROM ANY SCHOOL OR WERE YOU EVER DISCIPLINED BY ANY SCHOOL OFFICIAL? _____ YES   NO _____ : IF YES, GIVE PARTICULARS BELOW.

FINANCIAL HISTORY

67. IS YOUR LIFE INSURED? _____YES NO _____
VALUE OR AMOUNT _____ COMPANY _____ CITY & STATE_____

68. HAVE YOU A SAVINGS ACCOUNT? _____ YES NO_____
AMOUNT_____ BANK _____ CITY & STATE_____

69. HAVE YOU A CHECKING ACCOUNT?_____YES NO _____
AMOUNT_____ BANK _____ CITY & STATE_____

70. DO YOU HAVE ANY INVESTMENTS? _____YES NO _____
(stocks, bonds, etc.)
AMOUNT_____ COMPANY _____ CITY & STATE_____

71. DO YOU OWN OR ARE YOU BUYING YOUR OWN HOME? _____ YES NO _____
AMOUNT INVESTED _____ BANK OR COMPANY _____
CITY & STATE_____

72. DO YOU OWN OR ARE YOU BUYING OTHER REAL ESTATE? _____YES NO _____
AMOUNT INVESTED _____ BANK OR COMPANY_____
CITY & STATE _____

73. DO YOU OWN OR ARE YOU BUYING AN AUTOMOBILE? _____YES NO _____
AMOUNT INVESTED_____ AMOUNT OWING_____ MAKE_____ YEAR_____LICENSE_____

74. WHAT INCOME OTHER THAN SALARY DO YOU HAVE AT PRESENT? INCLUDE WIFE'S SALARY.
_____
_____

75. HOW MANY PERSONS ARE DEPENDENT UPON YOU FOR SUPPORT?_____

CREDIT HISTORY

76. LIST FIRMS WITH WHICH YOU HAVE, OR HAVE HAD, CHARGE ACCOUNTS. LIST FIRMS FROM WHOM
YOU HAVE BORROWED MONEY FOR ANY PURPOSE.

TYPE OF BUSINESS:

_____
NAME of FIRM

AMOUNT:

_____
Street Address   City & State

_____
Date Opened   Date Closed

PURPOSE:

CREDIT HISTORY (Continued)

TYPE OF BUSINESS:

NAME of FIRM

AMOUNT:

Street Address   City & State

Date Opened   Date Closed

PURPOSE:

TYPE OF BUSINESS:

NAME of FIRM

AMOUNT:

Street Address   City & State

Date Opened   Date Closed

PURPOSE:

TYPE OF BUSINESS:

NAME of FIRM

AMOUNT:

Street Address   City & State

Date Opened   Date Closed

PURPOSE:

TYPE OF BUSINESS:

NAME of FIRM

AMOUNT:

Street Address   City & State

Date Opened   Date Closed

PURPOSE:

TYPE OF BUSINESS:

NAME of FIRM

AMOUNT:

Street Address   City & State

Date Opened   Date Closed

PURPOSE:

---

76. CREDIT HISTORY (Continued)

WHAT IS YOUR TOTAL INDEBTEDNESS AT PRESENT ? _____
WHAT DOES THIS COVER ?_____

HAVE YOUR CREDITORS TREATED YOU FAIRLY ? _____ . IF NOT, EXPLAIN _____

_____

HAVE YOU EVER BEEN SUED ? _____ YES   NO _____ . IF YES, GIVE DETAILS _____

_____

_____

CRIMINAL HISTORY

Answer all of the following questions completely and accurately. Any falsifications or misstatements of fact will be sufficient to disqualify you summarily. (Exclude Traffic Citations)

77. HAVE YOU EVER BEEN ARRESTED OR DETAINED BY POLICE ? _____ YES   NO _____ . IF YES, GIVE DETAILS BELOW :

CRIME CHARGED _____   POLICE AGENCY _____

DATE _____ DISPOSITION OF CASE _____

CRIME CHARGED _____   POLICE AGENCY _____

DATE _____ DISPOSITION OF CASE _____

CRIME CHARGED _____   POLICE AGENCY _____

DATE _____ DISPOSITION OF CASE _____

78. HAVE YOU EVER BEEN PLACED ON PROBATION ? _____ YES   NO _____ . IF YES, GIVE DETAILS BELOW :

_____

_____

_____

79. HAVE YOU EVER BEEN REQUIRED TO PAY A FINE IN EXCESS OF $25.00 ? _____ YES   NO _____
IF ANSWER IS YES, GIVE DETAILS BELOW. _____

_____

_____

80. HAVE YOU EVER BEEN REPORTED AS A MISSING PERSON OR AS A RUNAWAY ? _____ YES   NO _____
IF ANSWER IS YES, GIVE COMPLETE DETAILS, INCLUDING JURISDICTION, DATES AND OUTCOME.

_____

_____

_____

CRIMINAL HISTORY (Continued)

81. IF YOU HAVE EVER BEEN FINGERPRINTED BY A POLICE AGENCY OTHER THAN FOR AN ARREST, GIVE DETAILS BELOW. YOUR ANSWERS WILL BE CHECKED WITH THE FBI AND OTHER AGENCIES.

AGENCY _____ DATE _____ PURPOSE _____

AGENCY _____ DATE _____ PURPOSE _____

AGENCY _____ DATE _____ PURPOSE _____

DRIVING HISTORY

82. CAN YOU OPERATE A MOTOR VEHICLE? _____YES NO _____

83. DO YOU POSSESS A VALID OPERATOR'S LICENSE FROM STATE OF CALIFORNIA? ____ YES NO ____
OPERATOR'S LICENSE NUMBER _____ YEAR ISSUED _____

84. DID YOU EVER POSSESS AN OPERATOR'S LICENSE ISSUED BY ANY STATE OTHER THAN CALIFORNIA
_____ YES NO _____ . IF YES, GIVE STATE AND NUMBER _____

85. WAS YOUR LICENSE EVER SUSPENDED OR REVOKED? _____YES NO _____ . IF YES, STATE
WHICH AND GIVE REASONS_____

_____

86. WAS YOUR LICENSE EVER RESTORED? _____ YES NO_____ WHEN _____

87. HAVE YOU EVER BEEN REFUSED AN OPERATOR'S LICENSE BY ANY STATE? ____YES NO_____
IF YES, GIVE DETAILS _____

88. HAS YOUR LICENSE EVER BEEN PLACED ON NEGLIGENT OPERATOR'S PROBATION?
_____YES NO _____ . IF YES, GIVE DETAILS _____

_____

89. HAVE YOU EVER BEEN INVOLVED IN A MOTOR VEHICLE ACCIDENT? _____ YES NO _____
IF ANSWER IS YES, GIVE COMPLETE DETAILS FOR EACH ACCIDENT WHETHER COLLISION OR NON-COLLISION:

Date _____   Police Investigation? _____ Yes   No _____

Location: _____ Cause of Accident: _____

Injury or Non-Injury _____ Who Legally at Fault? _____

Date _____   Police Investigation? _____ Yes   No _____

Location: _____ Cause of Accident: _____

Injury or Non-Injury _____ Who Legally at Fault? _____

Date _____   Police Investigation? _____ Yes   No _____

Location: _____ Cause of Accident: _____

Injury or Non-Injury _____ Who Legally at Fault? _____

DRIVING HISTORY (Continued)

90. LIST BELOW ALL TRAFFIC CITATIONS YOU HAVE RECEIVED:

LOCATION (CITY)	APPROX. DATE	NATURE OF VIOLATION	PENALTY OR DISPOSITION

91. WHAT CHURCH DO YOU ATTEND?_____ADDRESS_____

92. NAME OF RABBI, PASTOR OR PRIEST _____

93. DO YOU TYPE? _____ YES   NO _____   How many words per minute? _____

ACQUAINTANCES

94. Fill in below the names of five persons not related to you, and not former employers or references, who are friends, fellow students, or fellow workers. Names listed should be those of persons who have seen you frequently during the past year.

NAME _____

ADDRESS _____ RESIDENCE PHONE _____

BUSINESS ADDRESS _____ BUSINESS PHONE _____

BUSINESS, OCCUPATION OR PROFESSION _____

IN WHAT CAPACITY IS THE ABOVE KNOWN TO YOU _____

NAME _____

ADDRESS _____ RESIDENCE PHONE _____

BUSINESS ADDRESS _____ BUSINESS PHONE _____

BUSINESS, OCCUPATION OR PROFESSION _____

IN WHAT CAPACITY IS THE ABOVE KNOWN TO YOU _____

NAME _____

ADDRESS _____ RESIDENCE PHONE _____

BUSINESS ADDRESS _____ BUSINESS PHONE _____

BUSINESS, OCCUPATION OR PROFESSION _____

IN WHAT CAPACITY IS THE ABOVE KNOWN TO YOU _____

REFERENCES (Continued)

NAME _____

ADDRESS _____ RESIDENCE PHONE _____

BUSINESS ADDRESS _____ BUSINESS PHONE _____

BUSINESS, OCCUPATION OR PROFESSION _____

IN WHAT CAPACITY IS THE ABOVE KNOWN TO YOU _____

NAME _____

ADDRESS _____ RESIDENCE PHONE _____

BUSINESS ADDRESS _____ BUSINESS PHONE _____

BUSINESS, OCCUPATION OR PROFESSION _____

IN WHAT CAPACITY IS THE ABOVE KNOWN TO YOU _____

REFERENCES

95. Fill in below the names of six persons not related to you, and not former employers, who have known you intimately for a substantial period, perferably more than 5 years. All persons to whom you refer will be asked to appraise your character, ability, experience, personality and other qualities.

NAME _____ ADDRESS _____

BUSINESS, OCCUPATION OR PROFESSION _____ YEARS KNOWN _____

BUSINESS ADDRESS _____ BUS. PHONE _____ RES. PHONE _____

NAME _____ ADDRESS _____

BUSINESS, OCCUPATION OR PROFESSION _____ YEARS KNOWN _____

BUSINESS ADDRESS _____ BUS. PHONE _____ RES. PHONE _____

NAME _____ ADDRESS _____

BUSINESS, OCCUPATION OR PROFESSION _____ YEARS KNOWN _____

BUSINESS ADDRESS _____ BUS. PHONE _____ RES. PHONE _____

NAME _____ ADDRESS _____

BUSINESS, OCCUPATION OR PROFESSION _____ YEARS KNOWN _____

BUSINESS ADDRESS _____ BUS. PHONE _____ RES. PHONE _____

NAME _____ ADDRESS _____

BUSINESS, OCCUPATION OR PROFESSION _____ YEARS KNOWN _____

BUSINESS ADDRESS _____ BUS. PHONE _____ RES. PHONE _____

NAME _____ ADDRESS _____

BUSINESS, OCCUPATION OR PROFESSION _____ YEARS KNOWN _____

BUSINESS ADDRESS _____ BUS. PHONE _____ RES. PHONE _____

96. I HEREBY CERTIFY THAT ALL STATEMENTS MADE IN THIS QUESTIONNAIRE ARE TRUE AND COMPLETE, AND UNDERSTAND THAT ANY MISSTATEMENTS OF MATERIAL FACTS WILL SUBJECT ME TO DISQUALIFICATION OR DISMISSAL.

_____

(Signature in Full)

_____

(Date and Time Completed)

97. This questionnaire, together with as many of the following as are available, should be delivered to the Chief of Police, Berkeley, California, for the attention of the Personnel Office. If any are not immediately available, they should be mailed in as soon as possible. No appointments will be made until all have been supplied.

1. ABOVE MATERIAL COMPLETED
2. COPY OF BIRTH CERTIFICATE
3. COPY OF HIGH SCHOOL DIPLOMA
4. COPIES OF HONORABLE DISCHARGE AND SERVICE RECORD

APPENDIX C
The New York Municipal Police Training Council Act, as Amended

The Municipal Police Training Council Act was enacted by Chapter 446 of The Laws of 1959 and amended by Chapter 320 of The Laws of 1960.

The Act, as amended, reads as follows:

Executive Law—Article 19-F
Sec.
480. Definitions
481. Municipal Police Training Council
482. Executive Director: Employees
483. Functions of Council
484. Action by The Governor
485. Functions, Powers and Duties of Executive Director
486. Legislative Intent in Respect of Higher Standards
487. Applicability of Civil Service Law.

480. Definitions

When used in this article:

1. The term "Council" means The Municipal Police Training Council.

2. The term "Executive Director" means the Executive Director of The Council.

3. The term "municipality" means any county, city, town, village or police district in The State.

4. The term "police officer" means a member of a police force or other organization of a municipality who is responsible for the prevention and detection of crime and the enforcement of the general criminal laws of The State, but shall not include any person serving as such solely by virtue of his occupying any other office or position, nor shall such term include a sheriff, under-sheriff, commissioner of police, deputy or assistant commissioner of police, chief of police, deputy or assistant chief of police or any person having an equivalent title who is appointed or employed by a municipality to exercise equivalent supervisory authority.

481. Municipal Police Training Council

1. There is hereby created within The Office for Local Government in The xecutive Department a Municipal Police Training Council composed of eight members, who shall be selected as follows:

(a) three shall be appointed by The Governor.

(b) two shall be appointed by The Governor from a list of at least six nominees submitted by The New York State Sheriff's Association, who shall be incumbent Sheriffs in The State having at least two years of service on The Law Enforcement Training Committee of such Association or having other specialized experience in connection with police training which, in the opinion of The Chairman of such Law Enforcement Committee, provides the Sheriff with at least an equivalent background in the field of police training; and

(c) two shall be appointed by The Governor from a list of at least six nominees submitted by The New York State Association of Chiefs of Police, who shall be incumbent Chiefs of Police or Commissioners of Police of a municipality in The State having at least two years of service on The Police Training Committee of such Association or having other specialized experience in connection with police training which, in the opinion of The Chairman of such Training Committee, provides The Chief of Police or Commissioner of Police with at least an equivalent in the field of police training; and

(d) one shall be The Commissioner of Police of The City of New York or a member of his department designated by such Commissioner and approved by The Governor.

2. The Governor shall designate from among the members of The Council a Chairman who shall serve during the pleasure of The Governor.

3. All members of The Council appointed by The Governor shall be appointed for terms of two years, such terms to commence on April 1, and expire on March 31; provided, however, that of the members first appointed four shall be appointed for one-year terms expiring on March 31, 1960, and four shall be appointed for

two-year terms expiring on March 31, 1961; and provided, further, that the terms of the two members appointed as Sheriffs or of the two members appointed as Chiefs shall not expire in the same year. Any member chosen to fill a vacancy created otherwise than by expiration of term shall be appointed for the unexpired term of the member whom he is to succeed. Vacancies caused by expiration of a term or otherwise shall be filled in the same manner as original appointments. Any member may be reappointed for additional terms.

4. Any member of The Council appointed pursuant to Paragraphs b and c of Subdivision 1 of this section as an incumbent Sheriff, Chief of Police or Commissioner of Police, as the case may be, shall immediately upon the termination of his holding of said office or employment, cease to be a member of The Council.

5. The Council shall meet at least four times in each year. Special meetings may be called by The Chairman and shall be called by him at the request of The Governor or upon the written request of five members of The Council. The Council may establish its own requirements as to quorum and its own procedures with respect to the conduct of its meetings and other affairs; provided, however, that all recommendations made by The Council to The Governor pursuant to Subdivision 1 of Section 483 of this chapter shall require the affirmative vote of five members of The Council.

6. Membership on The Council shall not constitute the holding of an office, and members of The Council shall not be required to take and file oaths of office before serving on The Council. The Council shall not have the right to exercise any portion of the sovereign power of The State.

7. The members of The Council shall receive no compensation for their services but shall be allowed their actual and necessary expenses incurred in the performance of their functions hereunder.

8. No member of The Council shall be disqualified from holding any public office or employment, nor shall he forfeit any such office or employment, by reason of his appointment hereunder, notwithstanding the provisions of any general, special or local law, ordinance or city charter. (Added Laws of 1959, Chapter 446, Sec-

tion 2; amended Laws of 1960, Chapter 320, Section 7, effective April 1, 1960)

482. Executive Director; Employees

There shall be an Executive Director of The Council who shall be appointed by The Commissioner for Local Government, with the approval of The Governor, and who shall hold office during the pleasure of The Commissioner for Local Government. He shall perform such functions and duties as may be assigned to him by the Commissioner for Local Government. He shall receive compensation and reimbursement for expenses within the amounts available therefore by appropriation. The Commissioner for Local Government may appoint such officers, employees, agents and consultants as he may deem necessary, prescribe their duties, fix their compensation and provide for reimbursement of their expenses within the amounts available therefore by appropriation. (Add Laws of 1959, Chapter 446, Section 2; amended Laws of 1960; Chapter 320, Section 8, effective April 1, 1960)

483. Functions of Council

1. The Council may recommended to The Governor rules and regulations with respect to:

(a) The approval, or revocation thereof, of police training schools administered by municipalities;

(b) Minimum courses of study, attendance requirements, and equipment and facilities to be required at approved Municipal Police Training Schools;

(c) Minimum qualifications for instructors at approved Police Training Schools;

(d) The requirements of minimum basic training which police officers appointed to probationary terms shall complete before being eligible for permanent appointment, and the time within which such basic training must be completed following such appointment to a probationary term.

(e) The requirements of minimum basic training which police officers not appointed for probationary terms but appointed on other than a permanent basis shall complete in order to be eligible for continued employment or permanent appointment, and the time within which such basic training must be completed following such appointment on a non-permanent basis;

(f) Categories or classifications of advanced in-service training programs and minimum courses of study and attendance requirements with respect to such categories of classifications; and

(g) Exemptions from particular provisions of this article in the case of any city having a population of one million or more, if in its opinion the standards of police training established and maintained by such city are higher than those established pursuant to this article, or revocation in whole or in part of such exemption.

2. The Council may, in addition:

(a) Consult with, advise and make recommendations to The Commissioner for Local Government with respect to the exercise of his functions, powers and duties as set forth in Section 485 of this chapter,

(b) Recommend studies, surveys and reports to be made by The Commissioner for Local Government regarding the carrying out of the objectives and purposes of this article;

(c) Visit and inspect any police training school approved by The Executive Director or for which application for such approval has been made;

(d) Make recommendations, from time to time, to The Commissioner for Local Government, The Governor and The Legislature, regarding the carrying out of the purposes of this article;

(e) Report to The Governor from time to time and to The Governor and to The Legislature at least annually concerning the activities of The Council; and

(f) Perform such other acts as may be necessary or appropriate to carry out the functions of The Council as set forth in this article. (Added Laws of 1959, Chapter 446, Section 2; amended Laws of 1960, Chapter 320, Section 9, effective April 1, 1960)

484. *Action by The Governor.*

The Governor, in his discretion, may adopt and promulgate any or all of the rules and regulations recommended by The Council to The Governor pursuant to Subdivision 1 of Section 483 of this chapter. When The Governor promulgates any rule or regulation recommended by The Council, he shall transmit a certified copy thereof to The Secretary of State, in accordance with the requirements of Subdivision 1 of Section 102 of this chapter, including a statement as to the effective date of such rules or regulations. (Added Laws of 1959, Chapter 446, Section 2, effective July 1, 1959)

485. Functions, Powers and Duties of the Executive Director

The Executive Director on behalf of The Commissioner for Local Government shall have the following functions, powers and duties, to be exercised with the general advice of The Council and, in the case of Subdivisions 1, 2 and 3 of this section, to be exercised only in accordance with rules and regulations promulgated by The Governor pursuant to Section 484 of this chapter:

1. To approve police training schools administered by municipalities and to issue certificates of approval to such schools, and to revoke such approval or certificate;

2. To certify, as qualified, instructors at approved police training schools and to issue appropriate certificates to such instructors;

3. To certify police officers who have satisfactorily completed basic training programs and to issue appropriate certificates to such police officers;

4. To cause studies and surveys to be made relating to the establishment, operation and approval of municipal police training schools;

5. To consult with and cooperate with municipal police training schools for the development of advanced in-service training programs for police officers; and to issue appropriate certificates to police officers, attesting to their satisfactory completion of such advanced training programs.

6. To consult with and cooperate with universities, colleges and institutes in The State for the development of specialized courses of study for police officers in police science and police administration;

7. To consult with and cooperate with other departments and agencies of The State concerned with police training;

8. To perform such other acts as may be necessary or appropriate to carry out his functions, powers and duties as set forth in this article; and

9. To report to The Council at each regular meeting of The Council and at such other times as may be appropriate. (Added L. 1959, c. 446, § 2; amended L. 1960, c. 320, § 10, eff. Apr. 1, 1960)

486. *Legislative Intent in Respect of Higher Standards*

In enacting this article, the Legislature intends that all municipalities of The State should be encouraged to maintain, to the extent possible, standards of police training which are higher than the minimum standards recommended by The Council and adopted by The Governor; and the minimum standards recommended by The Council and adopted by The Governor shall in no way be deemed sufficient or adequate in the case of any municpality the appropriate authorities of which have established or propose to establish standards higher than such minimum standards. (Added L.1959, c. 446, § 2, eff. July 1, 1959

487. *Applicability of Civil Service Law*

Nothing in this article shall be construed to except any police officer, or other officer or employee from the provisions of The Civil Service Law. (Added L.1959, c. 446, § 2, effective July 1, 1959)

General Municipal Law—Article 10

209-q. *Permanent appointment of police officers; Completion of Training Program*

1. Notwithstanding the provisions of any general, special or local law or charter to the contrary, no person shall, after July 1, 1960, receive an original appointment on a permanent basis as a police officer of any county, city, town, village or police district unless such person has previously been awarded a certificate by The Executive Director of The Municipal Police Training Council created under Article 19-F of The Executive Law, attesting to his satisfactory completion of an approved Municipal Police Basic Training Program; and every person who is appointed on a temporary basis or for a probationary term or on other than a permanent basis as a police officer of any county, city, town, village or police district shall forfeit his position as such unless he previously has satisfactorily completed, or within the time prescribed by regulations promulgated by The Governor pursuant to Section 484 of The Exectitive Law, satisfactorily completes, a Municipal Police

Basic Training Program for temporary or probationary officers and is awarded a certificate by such Director attesting thereto.

2. The term "police officer," as used in this section, shall mean a member of a police force or other organization of a municipality who is responsible for the prevention or detection of crime and the enforcement of the general criminal laws of The State, but shall not include any person serving as such solely by virtue of his occupying any other office or position, nor shall such term include a sheriff, under-sheriff, commissioner of police, deputy or assistant commissioner of police, chief of police, deputy or assistant chief of police or any persan having an equivalent title who is appointed or employed by a county, city, town, village or police district to exercise equivalent supervisory authority.

3. The provisions of Subdivision 1 of this section shall not apply to a city having a population of one million or more to the extent that such city has, by regulation promulgated by The Governor pursuant to Section 484 of The Executive Law, been exempted from the provisions of Article 10-F of The Executive Law.

4. Nothing in this section shall be construed to except any police officer, or other officer or employee from the provisions of The Civil Service Law. (Added Laws of 1959, Chapter 446, Section 3, effective July 1, 1960).

Rules and Regulations for the Operation
of
The Municipal Police Training Council Program
for the Basic Training of Police
Officers in New York State

I, Nelson A. Rockefeller, Governor of The State of New York, pursuant to Section 484 of Article 19-F of The Executive Law, do hereby promulgate the following regulations in connection with the legislative enactment known as "The Municipal Police Training Council Act," the same being contained in Chapter 446 of The Laws of 1959, amending The Executive Law by the addition of Article 19-F, and amending Article 10 of The General Municipal Law by addition thereto of a new section, known as Section 209-q.

Therefore, be it known that the following regulations shall become effective on July 1, 1960:

Municipal Police Training Council Regulations Governing Practice and Procedure

Adopted	January 5, 1960
Effective	July 1, 1960

Regulations, recommended by The Municipal Police Training Council, promulgated by Nelson A. Rockefeller, as Governor of The State of New York, pursuant to Section 484 of Article 19-F of The Executive Law:

1. Definitions

a. The term "Council" means The Municipal Police Training Council.

b. The term "Director" means The Director or other head of a police training school.

c. The term "Executive Director" means The Executive Director of The Municipal Police Training Council.

d. The term "Basic Course" means the 80-hour course of train-as prescribed in Section two (2) of these regulations or a course which has been approved by The Executive Director, in writing, as meeting or exceeding, the minimum standards prescribed in Section two (2) of these regulations.

e. The term "municipality" means any county, city, town, village or police district in The State.

f. The term "police officer" means a member of a police force or other organization of a municipality who is responsible for the prevention and detection of crime and the enforcement of the general criminal laws of The State, but shall not include any person serving as such solely by virtue of his occupying any other office or position, nor shall such term include a sheriff, under-sheriff, commissioner of police, deputy or assistant commissioner of police or any person having an equivalent title who is appointed or employed by a municipality to exercise equivalent supervisory authority.

g. The term "school" means any training school exclusively for police officers as certified by The Executive Director of The Municipal Police Training Council.

2. *Municipal Police Basic Training Program*

a. *Statement of purpose:* It shall be clearly understood that The Basic Course described in Sub-Section (b) is designed as an absolute minimum program. Police Departments are encouraged to exceed this minimum program wherever possible. Regular in-service training beyond The Basic Course is strongly recommended for all police officers.

Nothing in this regulation shall limit or be construed as limiting the power of the civil service commission, police department or other agency or department of any county, city, town, village or police district to enact rules and regulations which establish a higher standard of training above the minimum required by this regulation, or which provide for the termination of the services of unsatisfactory employees during or upon completion of the prescribed probationary period.

No person shall receive permanent appointment as a police officer who has not satisfactorily completed the course of training and instruction required by the appropriate authorities of the municipality providing further that such course of training shall not be less than the minimum training requirements set forth under the provisions of Chapter 446 of The Laws of 1959.

3. *Certification of Schools*

A Director proposing a school shall file with The Executive Director at least thirty days in advance of the school a copy of the program listing the location of the school and the subjects to be given, and identifying the instructors for each subject. All instructors must be qualified by background, training and experience. The Executive Director may require any additional information to establish the competence of an instructor or for any other pertinent purpose.

The Executive Director shall then make an individual written certification for a school when in his judgment the information furnished warrants such action.

Schools must be certified for each Basic Course to be given.

4. *Attendance*

Attendance shall be required of each police officer at all sessions of The Basic Course except for valid reason. The Director of the local training school is authorized to determine the validity of absences of not more than 20 per cent of the hours of instruction. An absentee from any scheduled class session shall make up such absence as required by The Director. However, no police officer may be certified without receiving the full eight hours of instruction in Firearms.

A police officer who has been absent for more than sixteen hours of instruction and who desires to apply for certification by The Executive Director may appeal to him in writing, forwarding therewith a statement by the local Director together with sufficient supporting information by which The Executive Director may judge the merits of the appeal.

The Director shall be responsible for maintaining an accurate record of attendance for each police officer at The Basic Course. He shall retain such records for one year during which time they shall be available for the inspection of members of The Council or The Executive Director.

5 Notebook

Each police officer in The Basic Course shall maintain, as one of the requirements for certification, an adequate notebook during the course and shall submit such notebook to The Director. The notebook shall contain appropriate entries of pertinent material covered during the classroom sessions of The Basic Course. Among the factors to be evaluated in the notebook are: sufficiency of course content, organization, appropriateness of material, regularity of entries, neatness, accuracy and legibility.

6. Examination

A two-hour final examination must be taken and passed by each police officer for certification. The assembling of examination material, the giving and supervising of the examination, and the grading of examination papers shall be the responsibility of The Director. The Director shall retain the examination papers for one year during which time they shall be available for the inspection of members of The Council or The Executive Director.

7. Time Limits for Completion of Basic Course

No person shall, after July 1, 1960, receive an original appointment on a permanent basis as a police officer unless such person has previously been awarded a certificate by The Executive Director attesting to his satisfactory completion of The Basic Course.

Every person who is appointed as a police officer between July 1, 1960 and June 30, 1961, on other than a permanent basis, shall forfeit his position as such unless he has received, or within one year from the time of his appointment receives, a certificate from The Executive Director attesting to his satisfactory completion of The Basic Course.

Every person who is appointed as a police officer after June 30, 1961, on other than a permanent basis, shall forfeit his position as such unless he has received or, within six months from the time of his appointment receives, a certificate from The Executive Director attesting to his satisfactory completion of The Basic Course.

This regulation shall not be construed to preclude a municipality from establishing time limits for satisfactory completion of The Basic Course of less than the maximum limits prescribed above. If a municipality had adopted time limits of less than the maximum limits prescribed above, such time limits shall be controlling.

8.   Certification of Completion of Basic Training Course

Upon certification by The Director showing that a police officer has satisfactorily completed The Basic Course, a written certificate of satisfactory completion may be issued to such police officer by The Executive Director.

Receipt of the certificate by a police officer shall be considered as fulfillment of only one of the conditions of probation and shall not be construed as a limitation of the discretionary power of the appointing officer to terminate the services of an otherwise unsatisfactory probationer.

Recommended by
The Municipal Police Training Council
January 5, 1960 at Albany, New York
Approved and promulgated
on this fourth day of February 1960
      Nelson A. Rockefeller
      Governor
      State of New York

Basic Training Course for New York
Police Officers

The minimum amount of training for which certification can be granted by the Executive Director shall consist of the following:

Length of Course.

One hundred twenty (120) classroom hours of instruction. A classroom hour shall be defined as fifty minutes of instruction plus a ten-minute recess period.

Allotment of time and subject matter

		Hours
1.	Registration, Orientation, Classroom Notebook	1
2.	The Role of Law Enforcement	2
3.	Police-Community Relations; Human Relations	2
4.	Police Ethics	1
5.	Racial and Minority Groups	2
6.	Laws of Arrest, Search, Seizure; Civil Rights, Civil Liberties, Constitutional Guarantees	8
7.	Code of Criminal Procedure	5
8.	Penal Law	8
9.	Vehicle & Traffic Law	6
10.	Traffic Control; Accident Investigation	6
11.	Laws of Evidence	4
12.	Physical Evidence	4
13.	Court Testimony	5
14.	Note-Taking and Report Writing	3
15.	Interviews, Interrogation, Admissions, Statements	3
16.	The Patrol Function	3
17.	Firearms	16
18.	Defensive Tactics	6
19.	Techniques and Mechanics of Arrest	6
20.	Emergency Aid to Persons	10
21.	Recognition and Handling of Abnormal Persons	2
22.	Youthful Offender Law; Family Court; Handling of Juveniles	5
23.	Examination	2
	TOTAL	110 hrs.

Options

Ten (10) additional classroom hours of instruction shall be added to the above total of 110 hours by any of the following options or combination thereof:

(1) Selection of at least ten hours' instruction from the list of Elective Subjects noted below; or

(2) Expansion of the above list of subjects from 110 hours to 120 hours; or

(3) Addition by the Local School Director of any other subjects upon approval of the Executive Director of the Municipal Police Training Council.

from above options	10 hrs.
Total Classroom hours required for certification (Minimum Requirement)	120 hrs.

Elective Subjects

ABC Law and Enforcement Procedures

Navigation Laws

Conservation Law

Investigative Techniques and Procedures—Gambling.
" " " " —Narcotics
" " " " —Vice

Probation

Parole

Civil Defense

Personnel Safety

Community Resources

Crowd and Riot Control

Police Communications

Driver Training

Care and Maintenance of Police Equipment

Instruction in such matters as Department Rules and Regulations, Local Ordinances, personnel policies and procedures, and any matters to be prescribed by the local authorities may be given entirely upon local initiative. No portion of the instructional time devoted to this part of the training shall be credited against the total of one hundred twenty hours of instruction.

APPENDIX D

California Law Enforcement Standards and Training Act

*Title 4. Standards and Training of
Local Law Enforcement Officers
Chapter 1. Commission on Peace Officer
Standards and Training*

Article 1. Administration

13500. Establishment of Commission on Peace Officer Standards and Training: Number of members: Appointments and requisites: Terms. There is in the Department of Justice a Commission on Peace Officer Standards and Training, hereafter referred to in this chapter as the commission. The commission consists of nine members appointed by the Governor, after consultation with, and with the advice of, the Attorney General and with the advice and consent of the Senate, of whom five must be either sheriffs or chiefs of police or peace officers nominated by their respective sheriffs or chiefs of police, two must be elected officers or chief administrative officers of cities in this State, and two must be elected officers or chief administrative officers of counties in this State, as well as the Attorney General, who shall be an ex officio member of the commission. Of the members first appointed by the Governor, three shall be appointed for a term of one year, three for a term of two years, and three for a term of three years. Their successors shall serve for a term of three years and until appointment and qualification of their successors, each term to commence on the expiration date of the term of the predecessor.

13501. Selection of chairman and vice-chairman: Quorum: Summons of first meeting. The commission shall select a chairman and a vice chairman from among its members. Five members of the commission shall constitute a quorum. The Attorney General shall summon the commission to its first meeting.

13502. Compensation and expenses of members. Members of the commission shall receive no compensation, but shall be reimbursed for their actual and necessary travel expenses incurred in the performance of their duties. For purposes of compensation, attendance at meetings of the commission shall be deemed performance by a member of the duties of his local governmental employment.

13503. Powers of commission. In carrying out its duties and responsibilities, the commission shall have all of the following powers:

(a) To meet at such times and places as it may deem proper;

(b) To employ an executive secretary and, pursuant to civil service, such clerical and technical assistants as may be necessary;

(c) To contract with other such agencies, public or private, or persons as it deems necessary, for the rendition and affording of such services, facilities, studies, and reports of the commission as will best assist it to carry out its duties and responsibilities;

(d) To co-operate with and to secure the co-operation of county, city, city and county, and other local law enforcement agencies in investigating any matter within the scope of it duties and responsibilities, and in performing its other functions;

(e) To co-operate with and secure the co-operation of every department, agency, or instrumentality in the State Government;

(f) To do any and all things necessary or convenient to enable it fully and adequately to perform its duties and to exercise the power granted to it.

13504. Services of personnel in Department of Justice. The Attorney General shall, so far as compatible with other demands upon the personnel in the Department of Justice, make available to the commission the services of such personnel to assist the commission in the execution of the duties imposed upon it by this chapter.

13505. Expenditure of funds for training local law enforcement officers; purposes. In exercising its functions the commission shall endeavor to minimize costs of administration, so that the greatest possible proportion of the funds available to it shall be expended for the purposes of providing training for local law enforcement officers. All expenses for the operation of the commission shall be a proper charge against the revenue accruing under the provisions of Article 3 (commencing with Section 13520).

13506. Regulations. The commission may adopt such regulations as are necessary to carry out the purposes of this chapter.

Article 2. Standards for Recruitment and Training

13510. Adoption and amendment of rules establishing minimum standards. For the purpose of raising the level of competence of local law enforcement officers, the commission shall adopt, and may, from time to time amend, rules establishing minimum standards, relating to physical, mental, and moral fitness, which shall govern the recruitment of any city police officers or peace officer members of a county sheriff's office, in any city, county, or city and county receiving state aid pursuant to this chapter, and shall adopt, and may, from time to time amend, rules establishing minimum standards for training of city police officers and peace officer members of county sheriff's offices, which shall apply to those cities, counties, and cities and counties receiving state aid pursuant to this chapter. All such rules shall be adopted and amended pursuant to the Administrative Procedure Act (Chapter 4, commencing at Section 11370, and Chapter 5, commencing at Section 11500, of Part 1, Division 3, Title 2 of the Government Code).

13511. Places of training. In establishing standards for training, the commission may, so far as consistent with the purposes of this chapter, permit required training to be obtained at existing institutions approved by the commission.

13512. Inquiries by commission: Adherence to standards. The commission shall make such inquiries as may be necessary to determine whether every city, county, and city and county receiving state aid pursuant to this chapter is adhering to the standards for recruitment and training established pursuant to this chapter.

Article 3. Peace Officers Training Fund and Allocations Therefrom

13520. Creation of Peace Officers' Training Fund. There is hereby created in the State Treasury a Peace Officers' Training Fund, which is hereby appropriated, without regard to fiscal years, exclusively for costs of administration and for grants to local governments pursuant to this chapter.

13521. Levy of penalty assessment: Deposit in Peace Officers'

Training Fund. On and after the effective date of this section, there shall be levied a penalty assessment in an amount equal to 5 percent of every fine, penalty, and forfeiture imposed and collected by the courts for criminal offenses, other than a fine, penalty or forfeiture for a violation of the Vehicle Code or for any local ordinance relating to the stopping, standing, parking, or operation of a vehicle, and other than for a violation of the Fish and Game Code. When a fine is suspended, in whole or in part, the penalty assessment shall be reduced in proportion to the suspension.

When any deposit of bail is made for an offense to which this section applies, the person making such deposit shall also deposit a sufficient amount to include the assessment prescribed in this section for forfeited bail. If bail is forfeited, the amount of such assessment shall be transmitted by the clerk of the court to the county treasury and thence to the State Treasury pursuant to this section. If bail is returned, the assessment made thereon pursuant to this section shall also be returned.

After a determination by the court of the amount due, the clerk of the court shall collect the same and transmit it to the county treasury. It shall then be transmitted to the State Treasury to be deposited in the Peace Officers' Training Fund. The transmission to the State Treausry shall be carried out in the same manner as fines collected for the State by a county.

In any case where a person convicted of any offense to which this section applies is imprisoned until the fine is satisfied, the judge may waive all or any part of the penalty assessment the payment of which would work a hardship on the person convicted or his immediate family.

13522. Application for aid: Certification of adherence to standards for recruitment and training. Any city, county, or city and county which desires to receive state aid pursuant to this chapter shall make application to the commission for such aid. The application must be accompanied by a certified copy of an ordinance adopted by its governing body providing that while receiving any state aid pursuant to this chapter, the city, county or city and county will adhere to the standards for recruitment and training established by the commission. The application shall contain such information as the commission may request.

13523. Allocations. The commission shall annually allocate and the State Treasurer shall pay from the Peace Officers' Training Fund to each city, county, and city and county which has applied and qualified for aid pursuant to this chapter a sum which will reimburse the city, county, or city and county in an amount not to exceed one-half of the salary paid to each peace officer meeting the recruitment standards and participating in training meeting the standards prescribed pursuant to this chapter, during the period covered by the allocation, plus one-half of necessary living expenses incurred by such officer which are necessitated by training requiring that he be away from his residence overnight. If the moneys in the Peace Officers' Training Fund budgeted by the commission for such salary reimbursement are insufficient to allocate such amount to each participating city, county, and city and county, the amount allocated to each shall be reduced proportionately. In no event shall any allocation be made to any city, county, or city and county which has not, throughout the period covered by the allocation, adhered to the recruitment and training standards established by the commission as applicable to personnel recruited or trained by such city, county, or city and county during such period.
(Added by Statutes, 1959)

The rules and regulations of the Commission on Peace Officer Standards and Training are established in compliance with Sections 13506 and 13510 of the Penal Code of California.

Rules and Regulations

The rules and regulations have been adopted purusant to the Administrative Procedure Act as set forth in Section 13510 of the Penal Code and are effective on October 23, 1960.

1000. Objectives.

To raise the level of competence of local law enforcement officers by establishing minimum standards relating to physical, mental and moral fitness which shall govern the recruitment of any city police officers or peace officer members of a county sheriff's office; and, by establishing minimum standards for training of city police officers and peace officer members of county sheriff's offices.

1001. Definitions.

(a) "The Commission" is the Commission on Peace Officer Standards and Training.

(b) "The Executive Officer" is the Executive Secretary of the Commission.

(c) "The Department Head" is a Chief of Police or a Sheriff.

(d) "Officer" is a city police officer or peace officer member of a county sheriff's office.

(e) "Aid" is the money allocated annually from the Peace Officer Training Fund as provided in Section 13523 of the act, to cities, counties and cities meeting the requirements of this act.

(f) "Department" is a police department or a sheriff's department.

(g) "School" is any school, college, university, academy or local training program which offers law enforcement training and includes within its meaning the combination of course curriculum, instructors and facilities.

(h) "Trainee" is a peace officer for whom state aid is claimed under the act.

(i) "The Act" refers to Sections 13500 through 13523 of the Penal Code of California entitled, "Standards and Training of Local Law Enforcement Officers."

1002. Minimum Standards for Recruitment.

(a) The minimum standards shall be the following:

(1) Citizen of the United States.

(2) Minimum age of 21 years.

(3) Fingerprinting of applicants with a search of local, state and national fingerprint files to disclose any criminal record.

(4) Shall not have been convicted by any state or by the Federal Government of a crime, the punishment for which could have been imprisonment in a Federal Penitentiary or a State prison.

(5) Good moral character as determined by a thorough background investigation according to specifications entitled, "The Personal History Investigation" published by the Commission.

(6) Graduation from high school or a passing of the General Education Development test indicating high school graduation level, or a score on a written test of mental ability approved by the Commission, and equivalent to that attained by the average high school student.

(7) Examination by a licensed physician and surgeon. Only those applicants shall be elible for appointment who are found to be free from any physical, emotional or mental condition which might adversely affect performance of his duty as a peace officer. The applicant's declaration of medical history and the physician's findings upon the examination shall be recorded on forms which shall include but are not limited to all of the items specified in the "Health History and Physician's Record of Health Examination" published by the Commission.

(8) An oral interview shall be held by the hiring authority or his representative, or representatives, to determine such things as the recruit's appearance, background, and ability to communicate.

(b) It is emphasized that these are *minimum* entrance standards. Higher standards are recommended whenever the availability of qualified applicants meets the demand.

1005. Minimum Standards For Training

(a) The amount of training for which aid and certification will be granted shall be a total of 160 hours of instruction covering the Basic Course.

(b) The Basic Course is set forth as follows:

(1) SUBJECTS:

(A) REQUIRED:	HOURS
1. Arrest Techniques	6
2. Collection, Identification & Preservation of Evidence	6

3. Court Organization and Procedures   2
4. Courtroom Demeanor & Testifying   2
5. Criminal Investigation, Basic   26
6. Criminal Law (Penal Code)   12
7. Defensive Tactics   8
8. Examinations   3
9. Field Notetaking & Crime Scene Recording   6
10. Firearms (Legal Aspects)   2
11. Firearms (Range)   8
12. First Aid   10
13. Interviews & Interrogation   6
14. Juvenile Procedures   6
15. Laws of Arrest, Search & Seizure   6
16. Law Enforcement Ethics   2
17. Orientation   1
18. Patrol and Observation   8
19. Public and Race Relations   8
20. Report Writing   10
21. Rules of Evidence   4

       142

(B) ELECTIVES:
1. Administrations of Criminal Justice   4
2. Boat and Small Craft Laws & Regulations   4
3. Citations, Mechanics and Psychology   4
4. Civil Processes   6
5. Classroom Notetaking   1
6. Crowd Control   4
7. Department Organization   2
8. Driver Education (Classroom & Field)   6
9. Fingerprints   2
10. Human Relations   2
11. Jail Procedures   6
12. Jurisdiction of Other Law Enforcement Agencies   4
13. Narcotics and Dangerous Drugs   6

14.	Police Records	2
15.	Powers and Duties of the Sheriff	4
16.	Press Relations	2
17.	Raid Techniques, Stake-Outs, and Surveillance	2
18.	Scientific Aids (Laboratory)	2
19.	Spanish for California Law Enforcement Officers	3
20.	Special Weapons Training (Range)	6
21.	Tour of Department and Local Government Facilities	2
22.	Traffic Accident Investigation	6
23.	Traffic Laws (Vehicle Code)	4
24.	Transportation of Prisoners	2
25.	Use of the Police Radio and Teletype	2

(c) The minimum required hours shall consist of:

   (1) Required subjects   142 hours

   (2) Any combination of electives   18 hours

       Total *minimum* hours of instruction required   160 hours

(d) It is to be noted that if all of the above subjects were covered in a basic course it would total 235 hours.

1007.   Examinations.

Written examinations covering subject matter in the basic course shall be required of all trainees.

1009.   Time Limit For Completion of Course.

(a) Each trainee must complete the prescribed basic course within eighteen months from the date of his appointment as an officer.

(b) Extension of the eighteen month time limit for completion of the course may be granted by the Commission upon presentation of evidence by a jurisdiction that a trainee was unable to complete the prescribed course due to illness or injury.

(c) An officer who has received a certificate of completion of the basic course cannot again be claimed as a trainee by any department regardless of transfer or re-employment by another department.

1010. *Certificates Issued to Trainees and Other Officers.*

(a) Upon successful completion of the basic course each trainee shall be awarded the official certificate of completion by the Commission.

(b) Certificates and awards may be presented by the Commission for the completion of training beyond the basic course. The qualifications for said awards or certificates shall be published by the Commission periodically. It is the objective of this phase of the rules to encourage *maximum* training rather than minimum training.

1012. *Certification of Schools.*

(a) The Commission shall certify those schools deemed adequate to effectively teach the basic course. The identity of each school so certified shall be published by the Commission.

(b) Certificates may be revoked by action of the Commission whenever a school is deemed inadequate. In such event the Director of Training of said school and all Department Heads who participate in the school shall be notified by the Commission. The school may be recertified by the Commission when it deems the deficiencies to have been corrected.

1014. *Application for Reimbursement.*

(a) A jurisdiction desiring benefits under this act shall provide the following information to the Commission, in writing, prior to the starting date of the required training:

(1) Full names and date of birth of all trainees.

(2) Name and location of school where training will be taken and the scheduled beginning and completion dates of said training.

(3) When less than the full course is to be taken the applicant will specify the subjects and credit hours to be undertaken.

(4) Name of the person directly in charge of the training course.

(b) Upon completion of training a claim for reimbursement be completed and forwarded on the form provided by the Commission.

(c) A copy of the local ordinance as required by Section 13522 of the Penal Code shall be filed with the Commission.

1016. Assistance Provided by the Commission.

(a) The Commission through the Executive Officer and/or the designated representative shall upon request assist departments and Directors of Training in administrative and training problems encountered in complying with the technical aspects of the act as well as the ultimate objectives of the act, i.e., raising the level of competence of the California Peace Officer.

(b) The Commission may periodically publish or recommend that other governmental agencies publish curricula, manuals, lesson plans and other material to aid local departments in achieving the objectives of the act.

State of California
Commission on Peace Officers Standards and Training
Sample Ordinance Guide
ORDINANCE NO._____
An Ordinance Accepting the Requirements of Section 13522 of the Penal Code Relating to
Training of Law Enforcement Officers

General introductory paragraph used by the governmental agency enacting the ordinance.

Section 1. The_____declares that it desires to qualify to receive aid from the State of California under the provisions of Chapter 1 of Title 4, Part 4 of the California Penal Code.

Section 2. Pursuant to Section 13522 of said Chapter 1, the (city or county) of_____while receiving aid from the State of California pursuant to said Chapter 1 will adhere to the standards for recruitment and training established by the California Commission on Peace Officer Standards and Training.

General paragraph used by the governmental agency setting forth the procedure for adoption, i.e., effective date, publication and similar information.

The Personal History Investigation

In compliance with Section 1002 (a) (5) of the Commission Rules and Regulations a personal history investigation covering the following specifications must be conducted of each recruit employed pursuant to Chapter 1 of Title 4, Part 4 of the California Penal Code.

The purpose of the personal history investigation is to find examples of any character traits in the applicant's' life which might prevent his becoming a successful peace officer. The investigation should be conducted by an experienced investigator and the results should be evaluated by the department head and/or hiring authority to determine whether the applicant should be employed.

The first step in the investigation is the completion by the applicant of a detailed personal history statement upon which the investigation will be based. The investigation should be strictly confidential and the last step should be an interview with the present employer following permission by the applicant. If the applicant lives, or has lived, in a distant community, a letter should be sent to the local law enforcement agency requesting that an investigation be conducted.

Some of the things to look for in the investigation are: Does he have an uncontrollable temper? Is he unable to stay away from alcoholic drink when things go wrong? Does he "go to pieces" when confronted by danger? These and other similar characteristics may be revealed only through the personal history investigation. Names of the spouse and close relatives should be checked through appropriate files to determine whether they have criminal records, are in prison or may be in any status or position which might adversely affect the applicant's obligations as a peace officer.

When reviewing the results of the investigation, it should be remembered that what has happened in the past generally will happen in the future.

The investigation should include a check of as many of the following sources as possible:

1. Military records from the service of the United States or jurisdictions therein.

2. Documents, including driver's license, high school diplomas or other suitable record of graduation.
3. All local police files.
4. Police files in all cities where the person has lived or worked.
5. State Criminal records.
6. F.B.I. records.
7. State department granting drivers licenses.
8. Previous employers.
9. All schools attended.
10. References and relatives.
11. Present and past neighbors and landlords.
12. Fraternal and social organizations.
13. Any other source which previous contacts show to be important.

Health History & Physician's Record of Health Examination

This requirement supplements Section 1002 (a), 7 of the Rules and Regulations. It is in keeping with the concept that in order to render proper service to his community a California Peace Officer must be mentally alert, physically sound and free from any physical defect or mental or emotional instability which might adversely affect his performance of duty. His personal safety and the safety and lives of others will be endangered if he lacks these qualifications.

Requirements:

1. Medical Examination. The medical examination shall be given by a licensed physician and surgeon.
2. Medical History. Each applicant must supply to the examining physician a statement of the applicant's medical history of past and present diseases, injuries or operations.
3. Vision and Hearing. The applicant shall possess normal hearing and normal color vision. He must possess normal visual functions and visual acuity not less than 20/40 vision in each eye without correction and corrected to 20/20 in the better eye and not less than 20/25 in the lesser eye.
4. Physician's Findings and Record. The physician shall record

his findings on appropriate forms and shall note thereon, for evaluation by the hiring authority, any past or present physical defects, diseases, injuries, operations or indications of mental or emotional instability. The completed form shall be retained by the local jurisdiction.

Application for Reimbursement

1. Submit *in duplicate* for each trainee *prior* to date the course begins.
2. Jurisdiction .... Date ....
   (City or County)
3. Ordinance .... was adopted pursuant to 13522 **P. C.**
   (Number)
   on ....
   (Date)
4. Trainee's Name .... Date of Birth
   (Last, first, middle)
   ....
5. School...... ....
   (Date course begins) (Date course ends)
6. Date of Appointment...... 7. Trainee's hourly wage $......
8. 50% of estimated living costs per Commission bulletin dated May 16, 1961, "Policy for Reimbursement of Salary and necessary living expenses" $..........

Certification

I hereby certify that the trainee named herein was employed by this jurisdiction in conformance with the rules and regulations of the Commission on Peace Officer Standards and Training. This application is furnished pursuant to Section 1014 of the rules and regulations.

.... By....................
(City or County)   (Authorized Signature)
....
(Date)   (Title)
Trainee's Name ....
(Last, first, middle)

Claim for Reimbursement —
Peace Officers' Training Fund
(submit in triplicate)

Claimant: .... Date: ....

(City and/or County)

Total number of officers covered in this claim   ....

Reimbursable wages paid by claimant $............

Reimbursable living costs paid by claimant $............

Total reimbursable claim $............

Certification

I hereby certify under penalty of perjury: that I am the duly authorized official of the herein named claimant; that the claim is in all respects true, correct, and has not heretofore been paid, and is in accordance with law; that each of the officers listed on Attachment A has been employed by this jurisdiction in conformance with the rules and regulations of the Commission on Peace Officer Standards and Training pursuant to Chapter 1 of Title 4, Part 4 of the Penal Code. Further that each officer has satisfactorily completed all of the subjects in the basic course established by the Commission and there is on file at this jurisdiction original documents covering records of employment, physical examinations, payrolls and receipts of living costs to substantiate this claim. I further certify that I have not violated any of the provisions of Sections 1090 to 1096 inclusive of the Government Code in incurring the items of expense referred to in this claim.

I hereby certify that I am the duly qualified and authorized official of the herein claimant responsible for the examination and settlement of accounts; and that the amounts claimed have been paid by the herein claimant.

By ....

(auditor, controller, clerk, or other official)

Date ....

....

(City and/or County)

by ....

(Authorized Signature)

....

(Title)

....

(Date)

FOR STATE USE ONLY

Amount claimed $........

(Adjusted.......) Amount payable & due this claim $........

Approved by .... Date ....

Bulletin

To: Distribution List "D."

Subject: Policy on Pre-service College Training

On March 2, 1962 the Commission adopted the following policy:

"Policy on Credit for Pre-Service College Training

1. Credit for pre-service college training may be accepted in lieu of the basic course described in Sections 1005, 1007, and 1009, providing said pre-service training meets the following requirements:

   (a) The training must have been completed at a college certified by the Commission.

   (b) The students' course of study shall include all of the required subjects and minimum hours set forth in Section 1005 (b) (1) (A) of the Rules and Regulations.

   (c) Satisfactory completion of the requirements for and the award of the Degree of Associate in Arts with a Major in Police Science or a minimum of 60 units in a Police Science Major leading to a Degree or a Police Science transfer course acceptable for entrance into a State College or University.

2. Within 60 days after the date of employment, the employing jurisdiction shall forward to the Commission the name, date of birth, date of employment and a copy of the Degree or college transcript for each officer whose training is claimed to have been accomplished under the provisions of this policy."

Comments

It is believed the Commission's Pre-Service College Training Policy is of great importance to California law enforcement for the following reasons:

1. The Commission's certification of a college police science course will insure cities and counties that the course meets all of the minimum requirements established in the Peace Officer Standards and Training curriculum.

2. Many small departments do not participate in the P. O. S. T. Program because they are unable to send men away from home to attend Police Academies. By accepting qualified Police Science Majors who meet recruit standards, they can now adhere to the training standards and thus overcome a major problem.

3. It is believed the Pre-Service College Training Policy will influence many departments and espcially small departments to raise their minimum educational requirements to two years Police Science training.

4. Many departments employing Police Science graduates may desire to send them through certified Academies as part of their training and personnel evaluation process. Departments requiring the additional Academy training will receive State aid from the Commission as provided in the Rules and Regulations.

5. College students meeting the requirements of the Pre-Service College Training Policy will be awarded the Commission's Certificate after being employed by Police Departments and Sheriff's Offices who have enacted ordinances and adhere to the Commission's minimum recruitment and training standards.

APPENDIX E
The New Jersey Act Relating to Training of Policemen Prior to Permanent Appointment
Chapter 56

An act relating to training of policemen prior to permanent appointment; appointments in certain municipal and county law enforcement agencies; establishing a police training commission; and providing an appropriation therefor.

BE IT ENACTED by the Senate and General Assembly of the State of New Jersey:

1. The Legislature of New Jersey hereby finds and declares that a serious need for improvement in the administration of local and county law enforcement exists in order to better protect the health, safety and welfare of its citizens; that police work, a basic adjunct of law enforcement administration, is professional in nature, and requires proper educational, and clinical training in a State whose population is increasing in relation to its physical area, and in a society where greater reliance on better law enforcement through higher standards of efficiency is of paramount need; that the present need for improvement can be substantially met by the creation of an educational and training program for persons who seek to become permanent law enforcement officers wherein such persons will be able, while serving in a temporary or probationary capacity prior to permanent appointment to receive efficient training in this profession provided at facilities selected, approved and inspected by a commission created for such purpose; and that by qualifying and becoming proficient in the field of law enforcement such persons shall individually and collectively better insure the health, safety and welfare of the citizens of this State in their respective communities.

2. As used in this act:

"Approved school" shall mean a school approved and authorized by the Police Training Commission to give a police training course as prescribed in this act.

"Commission" shall mean the Police Training Commission or officers or employees thereof acting on its behalf.

"County" shall mean any county which within its jurisdiction has or shall have a law enforcement unit as defined in this act.

"Law enforcement unit" shall mean any police force or organization in a municipality or county which has by statute or ordinance, the responsibility of detecting crime and enforcing the general criminal laws of this State.

"Municipality" shall mean a city of any class, township, borough, village, camp meeting association, or any other type of municipality in this State which, within its jurisdiction, has or shall have a law enforcement unit as defined in this act.

"Permanent appointment" shall mean an appointment having permanent status as a police officer in a law enforcement unit as prescribed by Title 11, Revised Statutes, Civil Service Rules and Regulations, or of any other law of this State, municipal ordinance, or rules and regulations adopted thereunder.

"Police officer" shall mean any employee of a law enforcement unit other than civilian heads thereof, assistant prosecutors and legal assistants, special invesitgators in the office of the county prosecutor as defined by statute, persons appointed pursuant to the provisions of R.S. 40:47-19 and persons whose duties do not include any police function.

3. Any municipality may authorize attendance at an approved school by persons holding a probationary or temporary appointment as a police officer, and any municipality may require that no person shall hereafter be given or accept a permanent appointment as a police officer unless such person has successfully completed a police training course at an approved school.

4. Notwithstanding the provisions of Revised Statutes 11:22-6, a probationary or temporary appointment as a police officer may be made for a total period not exceeding 1 year for the purpose of enabling a person seeking permanent appointment to take a police training course as prescribed in this act. No person shall be permitted to take a police training course unless he holds such probationary or temporary appointment, and such appointee shall be entitled to a leave of absence with pay during the period of the police training course.

5. There is hereby established in the Department of Law and Public Safety a Police Training Commission whose membership shall consist of the following persons:

a. Three citizens of this State who shall be appointed by the Governor with the advice and consent of the Senate, 1 of whom may be the Special Agent in Charge of the State of New Jersey for the Federal Bureau of Investigation or his designee. These members shall serve for a term of 3 years except that of the members first appointed, 1 shall serve for a term of 1 year, 1 shall serve for a term of 2 years and 1 for a term of 3 years.

b. The president or other representative designated in accordance with the by-laws of each of the following organizations; the New Jersey State Association of Chiefs of Police; the New Jersey State Patrolmen's Benevolent Association, Inc.; and the New Jersey State League of Municipalities.

c. The Attorney General, the Superintendent of State Police, and the Commissioner of Education, who shall serve while holding their respective offices.

6. The commission is vested with the power, responsibility and duty:

a. To prescribe standards for the approval and continuation of approval of schools, at which police training courses authorized by this act shall be conducted, including but not limited to present existing regional, county, municipal and police chiefs association police training schools;

b. To approve and issue certificates of approval to such schools, to inspect such schools from itme to time, and to revoke any approval or certificate issued to such school;

c. To prescribe the curriculum, the minimum courses for study, attendance requirements, equipment and facilities, and standards of operation for such schools;

d. To prescribe minimum qualifications for instructors at such schools and to certify, as qualified, instructors for approved police training schools and to issue appropriate certificates to such instructors;

e. To certify police officers who have satisfactorily completed training programs and to issue appropriate certificates to such police officers;

f. To appoint an executive secretary, to serve at its pleasure, who shall perform general administrative functions, and to fix his compensation;

g. To employ such other persons as may be necessary to carry out the provisions of this act, and to fix their compensation;

h. To make such rules and regulations as may be reasonably necessary or appropriate to accomplish the purposes and objectives of this act;

i. To make a continuous study of police training methods and to consult and accept the co-operation of any recognized Federal or State law enforcement agency or educational institution;

j. To consult and co-operate with universities, colleges and institutes in the State for the development of specialized courses of study for police officers in police science and police administration;

k. To consult and co-operate with other departments and agencies of the State concerned with police training;

l. To perform such other acts as may be necessary or appropriate to carry out its functions and duties as set forth in this act.

7. Except as expressly provided in this act, nothing herein contained shall be deemed to limit the powers, rights, duties or responsibilities of municipal or county governments, nor to affect provisions of Title 11 of the Revised Statutes.

8. The commission, at its initial organization meeting to be held promptly after the appointment and qualification of its members, and thereafter at each annual organization meeting to be held on the first Monday in February, shall select a chairman and vice-chairman from among its members, and shall meet at such other times within the State of New Jersey as it may determine. A majority of the commission shall constitute a quorum for the transaction of any business, the performance of any duty, or for the exercise of any of its powers.

9. The commission shall maintain minutes of its meetings and such other records as it deems necessary.

10. The members of the commission shall receive no salary but all members designated in subsection c of section 5 of this act may be reimbursed for their reasonable expenses lawfully incurred in the performance of their official functions.

11. The commission shall report at least annually to the Governor and the Legislature as to its activities.

12. There is hereby appropriated the sum of $25,000.00 to establish and maintain the commission.

13. This act shall take effect immediately.

Approved June 3, 1961.

APPENDIX F
The Oregon Act
Police Standards and Training

181.610 Definitions for ORS 181.610 to 181.690. In ORS 181.610 to 181.690, unless the context requires otherwise:

(1) "Board" means the Advisory Board on Police Standards and Training appointed pursuant to ORS 181.620.

(2) "Executive director" means the executive director of the board who shall be the Deputy Superintendent of the State Police.

(3) "Police Officer" means any peace officer except any member of the Department of State Police.

181.620 Advisory Board on Police Standards and Training. (1) The Governor shall appoint an Advisory Board on Police Standards and Training consisting of nine members. Each member shall be a citizen of the United States and a resident of this state continuously for the year preceding his appointment. Five concurring members may act for the board.

(2) The term of office of a member is four years, and no member may be removed from office except for cause. Before the expiration of the term of a member, the Governor shall appoint the member's successor to assume the member's duties on July 1 next following. A member may be reappointed once. In case of a vacancy for any cause, the Governor shall make an appointment, effective immediately, for the unexpired term.

(3) A member of the board shall receive no compensation for his services as such member; but, subject to any other applicable law regulating travel and other expenses for state officers, he shall receive his actual necessary travel and other expenses incurred in the performance of his official duties.

181.650 Organization of board; approval of claims; meetings. (1) The board shall select one of its members as chairman and another as vice chairman. The vice chairman shall act as chairman when the chairman is absent or unable to act.

(2) The chairman shall approve voucher claims for indebtedness or expenses incurred under the provisions of and payable from appropriations made for the purpose of ORS 181.610 to 181.690. Otherwise the board shall prescribe such terms, powers and duties

for the chairman and vice chairman as are convenient for the performance of the functions of the board.

(3) The board shall meet at least once every three months at a place and time determined by the board. The board shall also meet at such other times and places as the chairman shall specify.

181.640 Board to recommend minimum standards and training for police officers; inspections; accepting grants; information services. (1) In accordance with any applicable provision of ORS chapter 183, to promote enforcement of law by improving the competence of police officers the board shall:

(a) Recommend for police officers reasonable minimum standards of physical, emotional, intellectual and moral fitness;

(b) Recommend for police officers reasonable minimum training, including but not limited to courses or subjects for instruction, facilities for instruction, qualification of instructors and methods of instructions;

(c) Recommend a procedure to be used by a public agency to determine whether a police officer meets minimum standards or has minimum training; and;

(d) Make reasonable rules and regulations to carry out the duties and powers of the board.

(2) The board shall cause inspection of police standards and training to be made and shall report annually to the Governor a summary of status of standards and training of police officers in the state.

(3) To improve the competence of police officers the board may:

(a) Contract or otherwise cooperate with any person, agency of government for the procurement of services of property; or

(b) Accept gifts or grants of services or property; or

(c) Maintain and furnish to public agencies who employ police officers information on applicants for appointment as police officers in any part of the state.

181.650 Examination of police training programs and instructors; certification. (1) Upon application, the board or its authorized representative shall examine and evaluate any instructor or any police training program.

(2) If the examiner finds that an instructor is qualified under the minimum requirements recommended pursuant to paragraph (b) subsection (1) of ORS 181.640, the examiner in writing shall certify instructor as being qualified for such a term and upon such conditions as the board may prescribe.

(3) If the examiner finds that a police training program or any course, subject, facility, instructor or instruction thereof is qualified to satisfy any minimum requirement recommended pursuant to paragraph (b) of subsection (1) or ORS 181.640, the examiner shall certify the extent of that qualification to the executive authority of that police training program for such a term and upon such conditions as the board may prescribe. An individual complies with any minimum requirement of paragraph (b) of subsection (1) of ORS 181.640 when he receives training that is certified under this subsection as qualified to satisfy that requirement.

181.660 Application of minimum standards and training to certain officials and police officers appointed before August 9, 1961. (1) The minimum training recommended pursuant to subsection (1) of ORS 181.640 does not apply to the Superintendent of State Police or to any individual who is a sheriff, constable or marshal.

(2) The minimum standards and minimum training recommended pursuant to ORS 181.640 do not apply to any police officer appointed before August 9, 1961, so long as he remains so appointed.

181.670 Effect of minimum requirements under authority other than ORS 181.640. Compliance with minimum standards or minimum training recommended pursuant to ORS 181.640 does not except any individual from any minimum requirement for selection or promotion as a police officer under ORS 181.260 or under any civil service law, charter or ordinance for a county or city.

181.680 Annual Report. The board shall make an annual report to the Governor which may include the progress of the acceptance by public agencies of the minimum standards and training recommendations adopted by the board. The board shall advise any public agency which is to be commented upon in the annual report of the nature of the comments before the report is filed with the Governor.

181.690 Police Standards and Training Account. There is established in the General Fund of the State Treasury the Police Standards and Training Account. All contributions or other moneys received by the board shall be paid into the State Treasury and credited to the Police Standards and Training Account and appropriated continuously for and shall be used by the board to carry out its functions.

181.700 Legislative limits; use of funds. It is the intent of the legislature in creating this agency to provide for the coordination of training programs for police officers and to set standards. The moneys provided in chapter 721, Oregon Laws 1961, are to be used for this purpose primarily and are not intended to replace existing contributions to the functions outlined in ORS 181.610 to 181.700.

APPENDIX G
Model Police Standards Council Act Drafted by
The International Association of Chiefs of Police

Model Police Standards Council Act of

(Title should conform to State requirements. The following is a suggestion: "An act establishing a Police Standards Council; providing certain educational and training requirements for members of police forces; and for related purposes.")

(Be it enacted, etc.)

Section 1.- Findings and Policy

The legislature finds that the administration of criminal justice is of statewide concern, and that police work is important to the health, safety, and welfare of the people of this State and is of such a nature as to require education and training of a professional character. It is in the public interest that such education and training be made available to persons who seek to become police officers, persons who are serving as such officers in a temporary or probationary capacity, and persons already in regular service.

Section 2.- Police Officer Defined

As used in this Act:

"Police officer" means any full-time employee of a police department which is a part of or administered by the State or any political subdivision thereof and who is responsible for the prevention and detection of crime and the enforcement of the penal, traffic, or highway laws of this State.

Section 3.- Police Standards Council

(a) There is hereby established a Police Standards Council, hereinafter called "the Council," in the Executive Office of the Governor. The Council shall be composed of 15 members, as follows: Five chief administrative officers of local government police forces, at least 3 of whom shall be from forces maintained by incorporated municipalities; 5 officials or employees of local government who have general executive or legislative responsibilities with respect thereto so chosen as to represent county government and municipal government; (the head of the State police), 1 representative of higher education, 2 public members and the Attorney General.

(b) Except for the Attorney General and the (head of the State police) who shall serve during their continuance in those offices, members of the Council shall be appointed by the Governor for terms of 4 years: provided that no member shall serve beyond the time when he holds the office or employment by reason of which he was initially eligible for appointment. Notwithstanding anything in this section to the contrary, the terms of members initially appointed to the Council by the Governor upon its establishment shall be: three for 1 year, three for 2 years, three for 3 years, and four for 4 years. The Governor, at the time of appointment, shall designate which of the terms are respectively for 1, 2, 3 and 4 years. Any vacancy on the Council shall be filled in the same manner as the original appointment, but for the unexpired term.

(c) The Governor annually shall designate the chairman of the Council, and the Council annually shall select its vice chairman. The chairman and vice chairman shall be designated and selected from among the members of the Council.

(d) Notwithstanding any provision of any statute, ordinance, local law, or charter provision to the contrary, membership on the Council shall not disqualify any member from holding any other public office or employment, or cause the forfeiture thereof.

(e) Members of the Council shall serve without compensation, but shall be entitled to receive reimbursement for any actual expenses incurred as a necessary incident to such service.

(f) The Council shall hold no less than four regular meetings a year. Subject to the requirements of this subsection, the chairman shall fix the times and places of meetings, either on his own motion or upon written request of any (five) members of the Council.

(g) The Council shall report annually to the Governor and legislature on its activities, and may make such other reports as it deems desirable.

Section 4. Powers

In addition to powers conferred upon the Council elsewhere in this act, the Council shall have power to:

1. Promulgate rules and regulations for the administration of this act including the authority to require the submission of reports and information by police departments within this State.

2. Establish minimum educational and training standards for admission to employment as a police officer: (a) in permanent positions, and (b) in temporary or probationary status.

3. Certify persons as being qualified under the provisions of this act to be police officers.

4. Establish minimum curriculum requirements for preparatory, inservice and advanced courses and programs for schools operated by or for the State or any political subdivisions thereof for the specific purpose of training police recruits or police officers.

5. Consult and cooperate with counties, municipalities, agencies of this State, other governmental agencies, and with universities, colleges, junior colleges, and other institutions concerning the development of police training schools and programs or courses of instruction.

6. Approve institutions and facilities for school operation by or for the State or any political subdivision thereof for the specific purpose of training police officers and police recruits.

7. Make or encourage studies of any aspect of police administration.

8. Conduct and stimulate research by public and private agencies which shall be designed to improve police administration and law enforcement.

9. Make recommendations concerning any matter within its purview pursuant to this act.

10. Employ a Director and such other personnel as may be necessary in the performance of its functions.

11. Make such evaluations as may be necessary to determine if governmental units are complying with the provisions of this act.

12. Adopt and amend bylaws, consistent with law, for its internal management and control.

13. Enter into contracts or do such things as may be necessary and incidental to the administration of its authority pursuant to this act.

Section 5. *Education and Training Required*

(a) Police officers already serving under permanent appointment on the effective date of this act shall not be required to meet any requirement of subsections (b) and (c) of this section as a condition of tenure or continued employment; nor shall failure of any such police officer to fulfill such requirements make him ineligible for any promotional examination for which he is otherwise eligible. The legislature finds, and it is hereby declared to be the policy of this act, that such police officers have satisfied such requirements by their experience.

(b) At the earliest practicable time, the Council shall provide, by regulation, that no person shall be appointed as a police officer, except on a temporary or probationary basis, unless such person has satisfactorily completed a preparatory program of police training at a school approved by the Council, and is the holder of a bachelor's degree from an accredited institution. No police officer who lacks the education and training qualifications required by the Council may have his temporary or probationary employmnet extended beyond 1 year by renewal of appointment or otherwise.

(c) In addition to the requirements of subsections (b), (e), and (f) of this section, the Council, by rules and regulations, shall fix other qualifications for the employment and promotion of police officers, including minimum age, education, physical and mental standards, citizenship, good moral character, experience, and such other matters as relate to the competence and reliability of persons to assume and discharge the responsibilities of police officers, and the Council shall prescribe the means for presenting evidence of fulfillment of these requirements.

(d) The Council shall issue a certificate evidencing satisfaction of the requirements of subsections (b) and (c) of this Section to any applicant who presents such evidence as may be required by its rules and regulations of satisfactory completion of a program or course of instruction in another jurisdiction equivalent in content and quality to that required by the Council for approved police education and training programs in this State.

(e) After the effective date of this act, each candidate for employment as a police officer who receives passing scores on his employment entrance examinations shall have credits, as established by the Council, added to his total examination scores for studies which he has satisfactorily completed at an accredited institution of higher learning in a program leading to a degree.

(f) Each police officer who is a candidate for promotion also shall receive educational credits as determined in section 5 on promotional examinations.

Section 6. Police Training Schools and Programs: Grants Under the Supervision of Council and the State

(a) The Council shall establish and maintain police training programs through such agencies and institutions as the Council may deem appropriate.

(b) The Council shall authorize the reimbursement to each political subdiyision and to the State 50 percent of the salary and of the allowable tuition, living, and travel expenses incurred by the officers in attendance at approved training programs, providing said political subdivisions or State agencies do in fact adhere to the selection and training standards established by the Council.

Section 7. Appropriations

(a) Except as otherwise specifically provided in this Section, the

Council shall be supported only by appropriations made by the legislature.

(b) The Council may accept for any of its purposes and functions under this act any and all donations, both real and personal, and grants of money from any governmental unit or public agency, or from any institution, person, firm, or corporation, and may receive, utilize, and dispose of the same. Any arrangements pursuant to this subsection shall be detailed in the annual report of the Council. Such report shall include the identity of the donor, the nature of the transaction, and the conditions, if any. Any monies received by the Council pursuant to this subsection shall be deposited in the (State treasury) to the account of the Council.

(c) The Council, by rules and regulations, shall provide for the administration of the grant program authorized by this Section. In promulgating such rules, the Council shall promote the most efficient and economical program for police training, including the maximum utilization of existing facilities and programs for the purpose of avoiding duplication.

(d) The Council may provide grants as a reimbursement for actual expenses incurred by the State or political subdivisions thereof for the provisions of training programs to officers from other jurisdictions within the State.

Section 8. Severability

The provisions of this act shall be severable and if any phrase, clause, sentence, or provision of this act is declared to be contrary to the Constitution or laws of this State or of the United States or the applicability thereof to any government, agency, person, or circumstance is held invalid, the validity of the remainder of this act and the applicability to any government, agency, person, or circumstance shall not be affected thereby.

Section 9. Repealing Clause

All acts or parts of acts not consistent with this act are hereby repealed.

BIBLIOGRAPHY

AUBREY, ARTHUR S.: *The Officer in the Small Department,* Springfield, Thomas, 1960.

GERMANN, A. C.: *Police Personnel Management,* Springfield, Thomas, 1958.

HIGGINS, LOIS L.: *Policewoman's Manual,* Springfield, Thomas, 1961.

LEONARD, V. A.: *The Police Enterprise—Its Organization and Management,* Springfield, Thomas, 1970.

MOSHER AND KINGSLEY: *Public Personnel Administration,* Harper and Bros., 1941.

PARKER, W. H.: *Los Angeles Police Daily Training Bulletins,* Springfield, Thomas, 1958, Vols. I and II.

PERKINS, ROLLIN M.: *Police Examinations,* The Foundation Press, Inc., 1947.

President's Commission on Law Enforcement and the Administration of Justice, *Task Force Report, the Police,* U. S. Government Printing Office, 1967.

RANKIN, JAMES H., M. D.: Preventive psychiatry in the Los Angeles Police Department, Police, Springfield, Thomas, Vol. 1, No. 6, July-August 1957.

YORK, ORRELL A.: *Municipal Police Training in New York State,* Municipal Police Training Council, Albany, New York, 1961.

INDEX

A

Administrative officers,
  training of, 41
Age requirement, 8
Agility, 11
Alabama State Police, 26
Applications, audit of, 19
Application form, 14, 66
Aptitudes, 13

B

Background investigation, 14
Baltimore County Police
  Department, 26

C

California Law Enforcement
  Standards Training Act, 38, 100
California State Legislature, 38
Character, 14
Chief of Police, selection of, 5
  competitive examination for, 58
Cincinnati Police Department, 26
Civilians, use of, 56
Collateral elements of the police
  background investigation, 14
Command officers, training of, 41
Conditions of service, 56
Contract Law Enforcement, 39
Coordinated statewide recruiting, 17

D

Daily Training Bulletins, 43
Detroit Police Department, 26

E

Eastman, George D, 6
Educational background, 12
Entrance qualifications, 7-17
  age requirement, 8
  agility, 11
  aptitudes, 13
  background investigation, 14

character, 14
height requirement, 9
intelligence, 11
mental condition, 10
physical condition, 10
physical strength, 11
residence requirement, 15
weight requirement, 9
Examination, announcement of,
  fn 19, 64
Examination, written, 19

F

Federal Bureau of Investigation, 56
Fosdick, Raymond B., fn 4, 29
Fresno Police Department, 26

H

Hamilton, Ontario, Police
  Department, 26
Height requirement, 9
Honolulu Police Department, 26

I

Intelligence, 11
International Association of Chiefs
  of Police, 40, 46
  Model Police Standards Council
  Act, 124
Interview, preliminary, 18

L

Lateral mobility of police
  personnel, 53
Los Angeles Police Department, 21
  Daily Training Bulletins, 43

M

Mental condition, 10
Milwaukee Police Department, 26
Model Police Standards Council
  Act of the International Associa-
  tion of Chiefs of Police, 40, 124

131

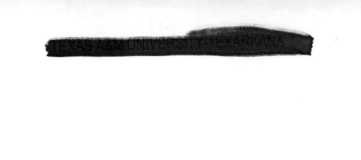